Comprehension Instruction
through
Text-Based Discussion

Linda Kucan
Annemarie Sullivan Palincsar

INTERNATIONAL
Reading Association
800 BARKSDALE ROAD, PO BOX 8139
NEWARK, DE 19714-8139, USA
www.reading.org

The International Reading Association attempts, through its publications, to provide a forum for a wide spectrum of opinions on reading. This policy permits divergent viewpoints without implying the endorsement of the Association.

Executive Editor, Publications   Shannon Fortner
Acquisitions Manager   Tori Mello Bachman
Managing Editors   Susanne Viscarra and Christina M. Lambert
Editorial Associate   Wendy Logan
Creative Services/Production Manager   Anette Schuetz
Design and Composition Associate   Lisa Kochel

Cover   Lise Holliker Dykes and Kelsey Louise Tyler

The publisher would appreciate notification where errors occur so that they may be corrected in subsequent printings and/or editions.

Library of Congress Cataloging-in-Publication Data
Kucan, Linda.
  Comprehension instruction through text-based discussion / Linda Kucan and Annemarie Sullivan Palincsar.
    pages cm
  Includes bibliographical references.
  ISBN 978-0-87207-497-2
1. Language arts (Elementary) 2. Reading comprehension. 3. Exposition (Rhetoric)--Study and teaching (Elementary)
I. Palincsar, Annemarie Sullivan II. Title.
  LB1576.K82 2013
  372.6--dc23
                                        2013003901

Suggested APA Reference
Kucan, L., & Palincsar, A.S. (2013). *Comprehension instruction through text-based discussion.* Newark, DE: International Reading Association.

We dedicate this book to the patient, earnest, and fearless teacher educators who contributed to its development. It would not exist without them.

CONTENTS

ABOUT THE AUTHORS

Linda Kucan is an associate professor in the Department of Instruction and Learning at the University of Pittsburgh's School of Education. She is a teacher educator for students pursuing an initial certification in elementary education and reading specialist certification, and a member of the Language, Literacy, and Culture doctoral faculty. Linda's research interests include vocabulary development, comprehension, text-based discussion, and supporting teachers' specialized knowledge building for comprehension instruction. She is also interested in tasks that support students' knowledge building and interpretation of texts.

Annemarie Sullivan Palincsar is the Jean and Charles Walgreen Jr. Chair of Reading and Literacy and a teacher educator at the University of Michigan. Her research focuses on text comprehension and engaging in knowledge building with text. She is also interested in the ways that children use language and literacy in the course of scientific investigation. Annemarie has served as a member of the National Academy's Research Council on the Prevention of Reading Difficulty in Young Children, the OERI/RAND Reading Study Group, and the National Research Council's Panel on Teacher Preparation. She is a former coeditor of the journal *Cognition and Instruction*.

PREFACE

This book is the outcome of research and teaching that we have been engaged in for many years, both separately and collaboratively. However, we mark 2008 as the pivotal year leading to the publication of the volume that you hold in your hands. In 2008, we secured a grant from the Institute of Education Sciences (IES) to develop resources for teacher educators to use in their reading methods courses (Kucan & Palincsar, 2008–2011). Specifically, we proposed to develop resources in the form of readings, activities, and video episodes to be used with preservice and inservice teachers who were learning about comprehension instruction. The resources would be designed to present discussion as the context for comprehension instruction.

Our motives were practical as well as personal. As teacher educators, we wanted such resources to use in our classes, but we couldn't find them. Useful descriptions and some resources were available related to reciprocal teaching (Palincsar & Brown, 1984, 1989), instructional conversations (Goldenberg, 1992; Goldenberg & Patthey-Chavez, 1995), Questioning the Author (Beck & McKeown, 2006; Beck, McKeown, Hamilton, & Kucan, 1997), collaborative reasoning (Chinn & Anderson, 1998), accountable talk (Wolf, Crosson, & Resnick, 2005), and quality talk (Wilkinson, Soter, & Murphy, 2010). However, we found that these sources were not specific enough to support the learning of the preservice and inservice teachers in our courses. When we applied for the IES grant, we approached a group of teacher educators and asked if they would be interested in working with us to create such resources. Our invitation was enthusiastically received by colleagues who shared our dilemma. (The honor roll of those collaborators appears at the end of this preface.)

The teacher educators' support was a key feature of our proposal to IES. That proposal was for a Goal 2, or development grant, which allowed us to develop resources through multiple cycles of design, implementation, and revision. A fundamental principle informing our grant proposal was that the development work would be carried out with opportunities for teacher educators to influence the design of the resources based on their experiences using them.

In the first year of the grant (2008), we developed an initial set of resources and introduced them to the teacher educators (take 1). They implemented the resources in their courses during the fall and spring semesters. We met in the summer of 2009 to talk about what worked and what didn't, as well as what was missing. Based on the suggestions of our collaborators, we revised the resources (take 2) and had them ready for use by the teacher educators in the fall and spring semesters of the 2009–2010 school year. Once again, the teacher educators convened in the summer of 2010 to provide suggestions about improving the resources. They shared their teaching logs, which gave us a sense of the time involved in using the resources as well as descriptions of how their students had responded to the suggested activities. Student assignments and assessments and course evaluations were other sources of information informing our appraisal of the resources.

Although we made revisions to specific readings, activities, and assessments in the resources based on the information described above, the basic goals of the resources remained the same: to provide both knowledge-building and enactment opportunities related to engaging students in text-based discussions for the purpose of mediating their comprehension and learning from text. We discuss how our efforts relate in specific ways to the Common Core State Standards (CCSS; National Governors Association Center for Best Practices & Council of Chief State School Officers, 2010) in Chapter 6. However, it is important to note here that our goals for text-based discussion are very much aligned with the emphasis in the CCSS on the "wide, deep, and thoughtful engagement" with texts that "builds knowledge, enlarges experience, and broadens worldviews" (p. 3).

Our work as teacher educators and our experiences working with teachers on a previous grant (Palincsar, Magnusson, & Spiro, 2003–2006) made it very clear to us that an essential aspect of supporting teachers' specialized knowledge building for engaging in text-based discussions was related to their understanding of theories of comprehension processes. A critical feature of that specialized knowledge is knowledge about text features and how they influence comprehension (Kucan, Hapgood, & Palincsar, 2011).

In our view, text-based discussion is an optimal context for mediating reader–text interactions for the purpose of supporting a reader's effort to build a coherent mental representation of text information. We see the effort to impose coherence on text information as the primary work of readers. The outcome of that work is what Kintsch (1998) referred to as a situation model—a representation of what the text means that is the result of organizing text information into big ideas and concepts rather than as a collection of discrete details and interesting facts. In a discussion, the process of building that representation is greatly facilitated by the social context in which the discussion is conducted. We explain our ideas about comprehension processes and the role of text-based discussion in mediating those processes for students in Chapter 1.

Our view of text-based discussion as a setting for comprehension instruction has its foundation in cognitive (Kintsch, 1998) and sociocultural perspectives (Vygotsky, 1978, 1934/1986) to which we have long subscribed. Our work with reciprocal teaching (Palincsar & Brown, 1984) and Questioning the Author (Beck et al., 1997) as well as our investigations of collaborative approaches to comprehension instruction (Kucan & Beck, 1997; Palincsar, 2003) demonstrated the positive impact of dialogical instruction on student comprehension. Current iterations of cognitive and sociocultural perspectives continue to inform our thinking (e.g., Graesser, McNamara, & Kulikowich, 2011; Kintsch & Rawson, 2005; van den Broek, Rapp, & Kendeou, 2005).

Research in teacher education has been another important influence on our thinking and on the development of this book. An article by Grossman and her colleagues (2009) provided a robust perspective for characterizing our work. They observed the approaches used to teach complex practices to seminarians, interns preparing to be clinical psychologists, and preservice teachers. Across these diverse contexts, the research team discerned three salient and shared features. First, across the three contexts, beginners were presented with representations of the complex practice; for example, preservice teachers observed in classrooms or viewed videotapes of classroom instruction. Second, beginners were engaged in decomposing the complex practices; for example, preservice teachers analyzed the process involved in planning for a lesson, such as determining the learning goals and activities that would support students in attaining those goals. Third, beginners had opportunities to engage in approximations of the practice. Preservice teachers, for example, planned lessons collaboratively with cooperating teachers and university mentors and participated in debriefing sessions in which their enactments were analyzed.

In designing the resources for the IES grant, we made use of the theoretical framework of representation, decomposition, and approximation described by Grossman and her colleagues (Kucan, Palincsar, et al., 2011). We also used that framework in developing this book.

In the chapters that follow, we represent text-based discussion as a high-leverage practice. As described by Ball, Sleep, Boerst, and Bass (2009), high-leverage practices are "teaching practices in which the proficient enactment by a teacher is likely to lead to comparatively large advances in student learning. High-leverage practices are those that, when done well, give teachers a lot of capacity in their work" (pp. 460–461).

We also represent text-based discussion as an optimal context for comprehension instruction, a representation shared by others (e.g., McKeown, Beck, & Blake, 2009; Wilkinson & Son, 2011). We acknowledge that discussions about texts can serve a variety of purposes, but our representation emphasizes discussion in which a teacher mediates reader–text interactions for two purposes: (1) to engage students in learning how readers impose coherence on text information (comprehension instruction) and (2) to support students in learning from text (knowledge building).

Our representation of text-based discussion is demonstrated in video episodes of teachers engaging in such discussions with students in classroom settings. Our work with video (Kucan, Palincsar, Khasnabis, & Chang, 2009; Palincsar et al., 2007), as well as the work of others (e.g., Rosaen, Schram, & Herbel-Eisenmann, 2002; Sherin, 2004), has demonstrated the potential of video to support teacher learning.

The discussion plans that are provided in Chapters 2–5 are also representations of text-based discussion for the purpose of comprehension instruction and knowledge building. Those chapters present not only the completed discussion plans but also the thinking informing the design of the plans. That thinking involves decomposing the planning process and using a framework to guide that process. Lesson planning was the focus of much research attention in the 1970s and 1980s (e.g., C.M. Clark & Peterson, 1986; Zahorik, 1970), and lesson study and lesson planning have recently become active topics on the educational research agenda once again (e.g., John, 2006; Lewis, Perry, & Murata, 2006). We see our emphasis on lesson planning as part of that active attention. We not only provide lesson plans and descriptions of the process of creating them but also emphasize the importance of enacting those plans. As such, we afford opportunities for teachers to approximate the practice of text-based discussion.

Those opportunities take the form of lesson plans for four different texts. The texts are available for free in their respective chapters of this book and on IRA's website (www.reading.org/General/Publications/Books/bk497.aspx) and can be duplicated and distributed to students. The lesson plans provide teachers with ways to engage students in discussing them. We also provide suggestions for videotaping or audiotaping discussions and offer a tool for analyzing the transcripts of those discussions. In our courses, engaging teachers in analyzing transcripts of their own discussions has proved to be a compelling context for supporting their learning about enacting text-based discussions (Kucan, 2007, 2009).

We also provide a set of tools that teachers can use in designing, enacting, and analyzing text-based discussions: a discussion planning tool, a text analysis tool, and transcript analysis tools. In addition, we provide a set of discussion moves, examples of prompts, cues, and activities designed to support student interactions with texts. These moves are included in the discussion plans and in the video episodes.

An important goal in writing this book was to limit our focus in terms of grade levels and text types. Specifically, we wanted to address comprehension instruction of expository texts suitable for students in the upper elementary grades, grades 3–6. We also designed this book with teachers as our primary audience. We hope that it will be used in teacher study groups, teacher education courses, professional development workshops, and literacy coaching sessions. We also hope that it will be a useful resource for teachers in building their specialized knowledge about comprehension processes and in implementing the planning and discussion of texts to support the learning of their students.

Acknowledgment

The work described in this book was supported by an Institute of Education Sciences grant, entitled "The Iterative Design of Modules to Support Reading Comprehension Instruction," that was awarded to Linda Kucan and Annemarie Sullivan Palincsar.

Our Collaborators

Teacher Educators

Judy A. Abbott, Stephen F. Austin State University

Jennifer Berne, National Louis University

Theresa A. Deeney, University of Rhode Island

Nancy DeFrance, Grand Valley State University

MariAnne George, University of Illinois, Chicago

Susanna Hapgood, University of Toledo

Susan McMahon, National Louis University

Ellen Pesko, Appalachian State University

Janice Marcuccilli Strop, Cardinal Stritch University

Teachers

Erica Hatt, Ann Arbor, MI

Max Weinberg, Chicago, IL

Reading Specialist Consultant

Debbie Dunn, Springfield, IL

Video Production Assistant

Kristine Schutz, University of Michigan

Advisors

Claude Goldenberg, Stanford University

Margaret G. McKeown, Learning Research and Development Center, University of Pittsburgh

Ian A.G. Wilkinson, Ohio State University

INTRODUCTION

We have designed this book to be six chapters and two appendixes. Chapter 1 provides an overview of current theory and research related to comprehension processes. The chapter also describes how theory and research have influenced approaches for teaching students how to engage in those processes. The concepts described inform the instruction that is presented in Chapters 2–5.

Chapters 2–5 present a sequence of four cases that focus on the discussion of four different texts, informational articles suitable for students in the upper elementary grades. The texts are short (4–6 pages) and can each be discussed with students in a 45-minute session. Two of the texts are science related ("Harnessing the Wind" by Mason James and "Coral Reefs" by Joanna Solins), and the other two deal with social studies topics ("Black Death" by Janet Callahan and "Jade Burial Suits" by Michael Priestley). Although the texts can be used in a variety of contexts—as part of thematic or content units—each can also stand on its own, offering students opportunities to learn more about important concepts that they will encounter again as they progress through school.

Each chapter begins with a careful reading and analysis of the featured text. Next, we present the process of developing a discussion plan for the text. Finally, we present a set of video episodes showing how teachers enacted the discussion plan with their students. The video episodes are integral to our plan for representing text-based discussion as a context for comprehension instruction. Each chapter has its own set of video episodes that involve the text that has been read and analyzed and used as the focus of the discussion plan. We indicate when to access specific video episodes in each chapter with this icon: 🎧.

In Chapters 2–5, we demonstrate how the planning process unfolds for each text and provide important tools to mediate that process: a discussion planning tool, a text analysis tool, and transcript analysis tools.

The **discussion planning tool** is a sequence of activities that make up the process of developing a discussion plan for a text. Those activities include the following:

- Careful reading of the text
- Analysis of the text
- Selecting learning goals
- Designing an exit activity
- Designing a launch
- Designing reader–text interactions, which are questions, prompts, and activities during reading

The **text analysis tool** is a framework for analyzing a text. That framework involves considering the text from three different but related perspectives. First, we consider the important content of the text. What are the big ideas that will allow readers to impose coherence on text information and develop a situation model (we explain what this means in Chapter 1)? Second, we consider those features of the text that would be useful for students to learn about and use to support their comprehension. Third, we consider if—and how—the text provides opportunities for students to learn about the disciplinary work of experts, such as historians, scientists, and archaeologists.

Finally, we provide **transcript analysis tools** (see Appendix A) that can be used to analyze a discussion of the text that we encourage you to enact with your students.

In addition to these tools, we have included examples of important **discussion moves** (see Appendix B). These discussion moves are questions, prompts, cues, and activities designed to support student interactions with text information. Specific discussion moves are used in the discussion plans for each text, as well as in the video episodes that show how each text was discussed by a teacher and group of students. We invite you to analyze those moves, and we share our analyses with you.

In Chapter 6, we place text-based discussion into a larger context, the current educational landscape in the United States and the Common Core State Standards. We also address features that contribute to implementation of text-based discussion in diverse classroom communities with English learners. This chapter addresses issues related to selecting a text for discussion, the teacher's role in discussion, and classroom norms that support a productive discussion context. Chapter 6 has its own set of video episodes that focus attention on establishing a classroom community that engages and supports student thinking and collaboration.

Although this book can stand alone, we have provided a guide that can be used to facilitate teacher study groups, teacher education courses, and professional development workshops. That guide is available as a free download from the IRA website: www.reading.org/General/Publications/Books/bk497.aspx. Also on that website are copies of the four texts featured in Chapters 2–5, which are also included in this book. Two of the texts—"Coral Reefs" and "Jade Burial Suits"—can be reproduced in full color.

Now that you know about the content of this book and the related resources that are available, we invite you to begin reading about and enacting text-based discussions in your classroom.

CHAPTER 1

Comprehension and Comprehension Instruction

*I*n his remarkable book *A History of Reading*, Alberto Manguel (1996) notes, "All writing depends upon the generosity of the reader" (p.179). This quote captures the essence of reading: Text is silent until the reader brings it to life. But how does the reader bring text to life? What determines the "generosity of the reader"? Why are some texts easier to bring to life than others? And, important for our purposes, how can teachers promote generous reading? These are questions that scholars from many fields, including education, psychology, and linguistics, have been working on for decades. In this chapter, we share their work for the purpose of describing how comprehension occurs and to identify the factors that influence comprehension. We then explain why talking about texts with learners is a powerful way to help learners better understand and learn from text.

Theoretical Models of Text Comprehension

In this section, we explain two current models of text comprehension and foreground their important contributions to understanding comprehension processes: the construction–integration model of text comprehension (Kintsch, 1998) and the landscape model of reading (van den Broek, Young, Tzeng, & Linderholm, 1999).

The Construction–Integration Model of Text Comprehension: Textbase and Situation Model

Cognitive psychologist Walter Kintsch (1998) has provided one of the most comprehensive and explicit theories of language comprehension in what he refers to as the construction–integration model of text comprehension. Just as the name suggests, there are two processes that are essential to comprehension: construction and integration. When we read, we use the information that is presented in a text to construct (or build) meaning of the text ideas. In addition, we integrate the newly constructed ideas with existing ideas that we already have regarding the topic. The product of this meaning construction is called a *mental representation* of the text. The meaning-building process begins with understanding words, phrases, and sentences and then involves integrating information in a paragraph, and across paragraphs and larger sections of text. This integration results in new learning, or new or elaborated knowledge. Readers can now draw on that knowledge in other contexts, whether reading-related or not.

Kintsch (1998) further elaborated that there are two possible mental representations of the text: the textbase and the situation model. He referred to the representation that results from the immediate sense making of the words and phrases in the text itself as the *textbase*. He referred to the mental representation that results from the integration of the textbase with prior knowledge as the *situation model*. Let's stop for a moment and consider the following paragraph from one of our sample texts, "Coral Reefs":

> From a distance, coral reefs can look like rocky underwater islands covered with plants. Get up close, though, and you'll find that the "rocks" are alive. Many of the "plants" are really animals. These structures are all created by tiny, simple animals called corals. (p. 1)

Even if a reader has never visited a coral reef, it is possible to construct a textbase from these four short sentences. In addition, the author urges readers, even within these four short sentences, to modify the textbase representation as new information is provided. As the reader moves from the phrase "from a distance" to the phrase "up close," the mental representation shifts from static, plant-covered rocky structures to structures that are actually teeming with animal life. The author uses helpful cues to support the reader in doing this. For example, the word *though* in the phrase "get up close, though" is a function word. It carries no meaning in and of itself but typically announces a contradiction (i.e., what you will see up close will look quite different from what you thought you were seeing from a distance). The use of quotation marks around the words *rocks* and *plants* cues the reader to alter the mental representation as well. It's as if the author were saying, "I might have referred to 'rocky underwater islands' in that first sentence, but those aren't rocks at all. And—guess what, reader?—those plants in the first sentence are actually animals."

A textbase for the sentences about coral reefs would include the ideas that coral reefs are made up of plants and animals that appear at a distance to be rocks covered with plants. Readers could construct a more or less complete textbase. However, there are multiple situation models that readers might construct from the same four sentences because the situation model depends on a reader's prior knowledge. If a reader has visited a coral reef, or seen photographs or videos of coral reefs, that reader would be able to use those experiences to elaborate on the text information, perhaps by remembering specific plantlike corals or the view a diver gets when approaching a coral reef. If a reader has no experience with coral reefs, or related experiences, that reader would be limited to constructing a textbase.

Constructing a situation model of text information is key to comprehension, and we make reference to this idea throughout this book. This idea guides our thinking about how a teacher should select a text, analyze the text, introduce it to students, focus a discussion of the text, and assess understanding of it. We feel strongly about this because constructing the situation model of a text is, in fact, the mechanism by which new knowledge is built through interaction with that text. Building knowledge, or learning from text, is the foundation for further learning and knowledge building, which in turn supports comprehension of new texts. As Duke, Pearson, Strachan, and Billman (2011) suggested, "knowledge begets comprehension begets knowledge" (p. 55).

The Landscape Model of Reading: Coherence

Extending Kintsch's model of text comprehension is a model referred to as the landscape model of reading (van den Broek et al., 1999). The purpose of this model is to answer the question, *How* do readers build a memory (or mental) representation of the text as they read? The landscape model is referred to as a computational model and was designed to capture both on-line processes (i.e., those processes that are directly under the control of the reader during reading) and the off-line memory representation after reading is completed. The model represents reading as a cyclical process, in which the ideas in the text fluctuate in their "activation." The sources of activation include the current cycle (or the interaction the reader is having with text in the moment), the preceding cycle, the memory representation of the text that has been constructed in the preceding cycles, and background knowledge. With each of these cycles, the memory representation is updated and, in turn, influences the next activation. The authors use the term *landscape* in reference to the fact that over the course of reading an entire text, information or ideas in the text fluctuate in their activation, creating a landscape of activations (van den Broek, Risden, Fletcher, & Thurlow, 1996). That is, the landscape consists of a series of peaks (active information) and valleys (information that is not the focus of active attention).

A very important contribution of the landscape model is that it treats the reader's goals and the reader's judgment about text coherence as central to the reading process. *Coherence* refers to meaningful connections among the various pieces of information that are available in a text. Coherence is the result of a reader organizing text information into a textbase or situation model. With each cycle, the reader makes judgments about whether the information that has been activated makes sense or whether additional activity will be necessary (e.g., rereading; studying a graphic aid, e.g., an illustration; consulting another source). Standards of coherence vary across readers and across reading situations, depending (minimally) on the purpose for which one is reading (e.g., for pleasure, to acquire a specific piece of information, to enrich one's understanding of a topic, to prepare for a debate) and on the characteristics of the text.

There are two kinds of coherence that play a role in most cases: referential and causal. *Referential coherence* is attained when a reader clearly pairs the reference for a person, object, or event in a text with the person, object, or event being referred to—for example, when a referent such as *she* is correctly paired up with Emily, the person being referred to. *Causal coherence* is attained when an event or situation has been explained to the reader's satisfaction. Every reader has his or her own threshold of coherence when approaching a particular text. This threshold is determined by, for example, the purpose for reading or the reader's interest in the topic. If the threshold is met, the reader moves on into the next cycle of on-line processing of the text; if the threshold is not met, then the processing of the current cycle continues. This means that coherence does not reside in the text alone but is a function of the interaction between the reader and the text.

Let's pause for a moment and apply the ideas of referential and causal coherence to the following excerpt from the "Coral Reefs" sample text:

> Coral reefs are important for many reasons. They support a huge diversity of life. Though they cover less than one percent of the ocean floor, they are home to about 25 percent of ocean species. That's more than a million different species! Humans rely on reefs, too. Reefs are home to fish that people eat. Reefs also protect beaches and coastal communities from pounding ocean waves during storms. They provide income for many people through the tourism they create. (p. 3)

There are several opportunities in this brief excerpt to examine referential coherence. Following the introduction to coral reefs in the first sentence, the author uses the referent *they* three times in reference to coral reefs. The referent *that* is used to explicate how much 25% of ocean species represents (i.e., 25% percent of ocean species is more than a million different species). If the reader understands the use of *they* and *that* in this text, then the reader has achieved referential coherence.

This brief excerpt also provides the opportunity to explore causal coherence. The author is making two arguments in this brief excerpt: The first is that coral reefs are important for many reasons; the second—and subsumed—argument is that humans rely on reefs. In each case, the author provides a clear explanation for the argument, or claim, made in the text. To bolster the claim that coral reefs are important for many reasons, the author cites the fact that coral reefs support a huge diversity of life. The author concretizes that fact by specifying that 25% of ocean species make their home in the coral reefs. The author further supports the claim about the importance of the coral reefs by stating that not only ocean species rely on reefs but also humans. To support that argument, the author provides three ways in which humans depend on coral reefs: for food, for protection, and for their economy. If the reader appreciates the argument building in which the author is engaged, or understands the claims–evidence relationships throughout this excerpt, then the reader has attained causal coherence.

There is another aspect of coherence that is worth our attention; that is, texts can be coherent at both a local and a global level. *Local coherence* occurs within small portions of texts, usually within texts no longer than a paragraph. Hence, our treatment of coherence, thus far, has been at a local level. In contrast, *global coherence* refers to the text as a whole. A text that exhibits global coherence supports readers in synthesizing information across paragraphs and in building a situation model while reading. Although researchers have often studied how readers attain local coherence, educators typically care more about global coherence. For example, as the reader proceeds through the text on coral reefs, evidence of building global coherence would be if the reader began to organize the text information describing the features of a coral reef over several paragraphs by thinking about it as an ecosystem characterized by the interdependence of its plants, animals, and environment.

We linger on the topic of text coherence because we want to make the case that text-based discussions are the ideal context in which students and their teachers can experience reading as a process of checking for coherence and building both local and global coherence. We argue that (1) the texts that lend themselves ideally to discussion are those that require work on the part of the typical reader to build coherence, and (2) the moves that teachers make in a text-based discussion should be guided by the goal of collectively building local and global coherence so each reader constructs both a textbase and a situation model of the text. It is through these processes that readers understand what they are reading and integrate the ideas in the text with prior knowledge and experience.

A Representation of the Important Elements of Reading Comprehension

The ease and/or success with which the reader imposes coherence on a text to construct a situation model is related to a number of elements not yet discussed in depth. These elements include aspects of the social context in which the reading occurs, the purposes the reader has for reading, the degree of motivation the reader brings to the reading, and specific characteristics of the text (e.g., its organization). To represent this complexity, the RAND Reading Study Group (2002) suggested that reading comprehension can be explained and supported by attending to the reader, the text, the activity in which the reader and the text are in interplay, and the larger sociocultural context in which this activity takes place. In the next section, we discuss each of these elements in more detail, beginning with the reader.

The Reader

Decades ago, Herbert Clark and Eve Clark (1977) proposed that a reader must bring both a mental dictionary and a mental encyclopedia to his or her reading. They argued that one's mental dictionary, on the one hand, provides information regarding words, with each entry having information about the word's pronunciation, syntactic category, and meaning. The mental encyclopedia, on the other hand, contains all the reader's world knowledge as it relates to the words in the text. So, a reader's mental encyclopedia entry related to the term *coral reef* might contain information about the appearance, function, origins, and locations of coral reefs. A reader must consult his or her mental dictionary *and* mental encyclopedia to construct a mental representation of a text. There are limitations to these metaphors, but they provide useful distinctions. For example, English learners may have mental encyclopedias that are chock-full, but their mental English dictionaries may not be up to the task of evoking useful entries from those encyclopedias. Similarly, a reader may have a lot of word-level information that remains at the level of a mental dictionary and is not being taken up and incorporated into the reader's mental encyclopedia. Perhaps the best illustration of how the dictionary and encyclopedia must be working in tandem is accomplished by considering how a reader makes sense of polysemous words, or words that have two or more meanings. The classic example of a polysemous word in the English language is *ran*, whose multiple meanings are represented in the following sentences:

- The battery ran down.
- Barak Obama ran for president.
- A brook ran through the meadow.
- The marathoner ran a personal best.
- She ran an errand.

Only by considering the context in which *ran* is being used is it possible to interpret the word accurately.

For cognitive psychologist Charles Perfetti (2011), who has made reading processes a focus for his sustained investigation, word knowledge is what makes it possible for readers who have decoding and word-level skills under control to comprehend texts. Knowledge of word meanings supports readers in understanding the phrases and sentences of connected text passages. That knowledge of word meanings is in turn enhanced and enriched by reading. Word knowledge and knowledge about ideas and topics develop in tandem. As a reader's knowledge expands with ideas and information for enhancing or including new mental encyclopedia entries, so too do the entries in a reader's mental dictionary. The importance of knowledge building for readers was emphasized by E.D. Hirsch, Jr. (2006), who noted,

> Content is not adequately addressed in American schools, especially in the early grades. None of our current methods attempt to steadily build up children's knowledge; not the empty state and district language arts standards…; not the reading textbooks, which jump from one trivial piece to another; and

not the comprehension drills conducted in schools….These all promote the view that comprehension depends on having formal skills rather than broad knowledge. (para. 5)

Since the 1970s, researchers have been exploring additional reader factors that predict or influence comprehension activity. For example, the interest or motivation that the reader brings to the reading influences the activity and outcomes of reading in ways you might predict: Students learn more from material that they find engaging or satisfying to read (Guthrie, 2004). Furthermore, the intentionality with which the reader reads the text, which may or may not be related to the reader's interest and motivation, also influences reading outcomes (Pressley, Johnson, Symons, McGoldrick, & Kurita, 1989). This line of research, which investigated variations in the ways readers differentially interact with text to construct meaning, gave rise to the agenda of teaching students to be strategic readers.

The Text

Whereas attention to reader factors has a long history in the reading community, less attention has been paid to the role that the text itself plays in influencing comprehension. This is not to suggest that reading researchers have ignored text factors. Years ago, Armbruster and Anderson (1988) called attention to the fact that some texts were written in such a fashion as to be inconsiderate of the reader, and Beck, McKeown, Sinatra, and Loxterman (1991) called attention to the role that seductive details could play in distracting the reader from constructing big ideas in the text. One useful way in which text can be characterized is in terms of its macrolevel and microlevel features. We review these features because they are helpful to thinking about both the resources that a text can provide in supporting the reader and the challenges that a text can represent.

At the *macrolevel*, a text can be characterized in terms of its genre, organization, and graphic and typographic features. Considering the genre of a text is useful because the genre not only tells the reader something about the content of the text but also about the way that content is put together. Genre is defined primarily by the purpose of a text, with the features of the text following from its purpose. Lists, recipes, romance novels, mysteries, and historical fiction are all examples of genres; each genre achieves a particular social purpose. The genre that we are focused on is informational text; knowing that a text is informational in nature should set up the expectation that the text was written to inform the reader about the natural or social world. Furthermore, the reader should generally be able to assume that the text was written by someone who is knowledgeable about the topic of the text. Additional macrolevel features, such as the organization of the text and the use of graphics and typographical features, are characteristic of informational text.

There is a range of text structures that characterize informational text. Problem/solution, compare/contrast, cause/effect, and chronological sequence are examples. Meyer, Wijekumar, and Lin (2011) have demonstrated that readers can be taught to pay close attention to the structure of a text and use that structure to support their recall of the text. Analyzing texts to determine their structure can also assist teachers in identifying learning goals and framing initiating questions.

In the chapters that follow, we provide several examples of informational texts with various text structures and characteristics. We also analyze each text in detail. We have already begun to explore the text entitled "Coral Reefs," and we explore this text further in Chapter 4. "Coral Reefs" is interesting because although its content can be characterized in terms of cause and effect, it is an example in which the effects are obvious, but scientists are still debating the causes. "Black Death," introduced in Chapter 3, is a text that has been prepared as a historical account (see information below). "Harnessing the Wind" (Chapter 2) and "Jade Burial Suits" (Chapter 5) are primarily descriptive texts.

A final macrolevel feature of texts is the inclusion of graphics and typographic features. Although we generally assume that graphics, which can take the form of diagrams, photographs, charts, and maps, are useful to extending the ideas that are presented in a text, they actually represent their own class of text interpretation challenges. Students may need support in learning to interpret a diagram and coordinating the information in the graphic with the information in the prose. The graphics included in our sample texts can be incorporated into text-based discussions in very productive ways. For example, in "Jade Burial Suits," a timeline of the ancient Chinese dynasties provides the reader with the most useful explanation for why the ancient Chinese stopped constructing burial suits. In "Black Death," a map is used to convey information about the sequence and timing of the spread of the bubonic plague across Europe. In "Harnessing the Wind," a diagram is used to explain how a wind turbine works. Typographic features include headings, which can cue the reader to the content and organization of a text, and boldfaced and italicized type can be used to emphasize the importance of particular words or phrases. Despite the potential usefulness of these features, most readers need support to experience that usefulness.

Microlevel text features include the organization of text into paragraphs and the use of main idea—or topic—sentences. However, the largest class of microlevel text features are the linguistic features of the text—that is, specific words that have a particular function in the text. Recently, linguists (e.g., Fang, 2006; Schleppegrell, 2004) have joined psychologists (e.g., Graesser, McNamara, & Louwerse, 2003) in turning their attention to analyzing texts for the linguistic features that influence the success with which readers can construct the textbase, construct the situation model, and strive for coherence. Referents, which we described earlier, are a primary example of a microlevel linguistic feature, but others include *connectives* that signal relationships among ideas in the text (e.g., *because, but, however, therefore*). We summarize important macrolevel and microlevel features of text in the tables below.

Macrolevel Features

Genre: Kinds of text	• Narrative: Stories such as folk tales, mysteries, biographies, and novels • Expository: Articles that provide explanations and information • Persuasive: Essays or newspaper editorials that present a point of view • Descriptive: Texts that create verbal pictures
Organization: Structures in which text information is presented	• Chronology, or the presentation of a sequence of events, often cued by words such as *first, next, then, finally*, which cue the reader about the order of events • Cause/effect: Cued by words such as *because, as a result, due to, as a consequence* • Problem/solution: Cued by words such as *the effect, is resolved, leads to* • Comparison: Cued by words such as *similarly, both, likewise* • Contrast: Cued by words such as *instead of, on the other hand, as opposed to*
Graphics	• Illustrations, photographs, diagrams, charts, tables, maps
Typographic features	• Typeface, such as boldface and italic, and type size
Graphic features	• Titles, headings, subheadings, sidebars

Microlevel Features

Paragraph conventions	• Topic sentences
Connectives	• Causal connectives; words that link a cause with an effect (*because, therefore, as a result*) • Temporal connectives; words that help put events in order of time (*then, next, before, finally, first, second, third*) • Logical connectives; words used to indicate reasoning and relationships between ideas (*therefore, in other words, furthermore*) • Contrastive connectives; words used to contrast ideas (*but, however, despite*)
Referents	• Pronouns or alternative ways of referring to a person or thing that has already been mentioned (*she, his, its, their, them; this, that; the journalist, the writer*)
Verb tense	• Indicates the time of an action, event, or condition by placing it in the past, present, or future
Repetition	• Repeating or reinstating an idea mentioned previously, especially repeating an idea mentioned in the last sentence of one paragraph in the first sentence of the next paragraph

In addition to pointing out important microlevel linguistic features of text, linguists are also calling attention to the domain-specific nature of linguistic features. For example, Fang (2006) has identified some of the linguistic challenges of the science texts that students in the middle grades are expected to interpret and learn from, including technical vocabulary with multiple morphemes such as *heliotropism*, as well as words such as *force* and *tension* for which students have acquired meanings that do not match the words' specific scientific meanings.

Whereas scientists typically develop theories about how the natural world works by systematically manipulating and documenting phenomena, historians develop theories about the past by reading documents and examining evidence. They look for corroboration across sources and develop arguments about human motivations. As Schleppegrell (2004) explained, "History is construed through a different kind of discourse than science. History is primarily a textual construction, and the foregrounding of interpretation gives history discourse its distinctive character" (p. 125). Historians engage in the writing of recounts, in which they retell a sequence of events; accounts, in which they explain, rather than simply retell, events; explanations, in which they explain past events by examining causes and consequences; and arguments, in which they advocate for a particular interpretation by presenting and critiquing a range of positions or arguments. There are particular linguistic features that characterize each of these genres of historical writing (Coffin, as cited in Schleppegrell, 2004).

In the chapters that follow, you will see ways in which we have been influenced by linguistic perspectives in the planning and enactment of text-based discussions. For example, we have noted contrastive connectives (e.g., *but, however*) in some of the texts and have modeled how teachers might call students' attention to the role these function words play in interpreting the text. Furthermore, we have made salient how teachers can use domain-specific features of a text as they plan and enact text-based discussions. For example, when reading "Black Death," in which the author engages in historical explanation, we encourage teachers to focus on the causal chain that the author presents in explaining events that transpired during the time of the bubonic plague. Furthermore, we encourage teachers to consider what sources of evidence the historians could draw on to reconstruct events that occurred hundreds of years ago.

The Activity

Activity in the RAND Reading Study Group's (2002) model was included to indicate that reader–text interactions do not occur in a vacuum; reading is done with a purpose—to achieve some end. Sometimes the purpose is determined by the reader, and sometimes it is not. Frequently, in fact, the purpose for reading in school is established by someone other than the reader. Activity captures the purpose, the operations in which the reader engages to attain the purpose, and the outcomes of those operations.

The activity can change in the midst of interacting with a text; for example, a reader who is reading about the jade burial suits that were used in ancient China may begin reading the text because she was told to do so and then become captivated by the topic. The outcome of reading because one was told to do so may be as shallow as finishing the reading, whereas the outcome of reading because one is captivated by the topic may be a sense of deep satisfaction, curiosity to know more, or frustration because the author left a number of questions unanswered. Ideally, the reader is processing the text mindful of a purpose for reading. Relating back to our earlier discussion, a reader with a clear and compelling purpose for reading is more likely to hold the text to a higher standard of coherence and to engage in processes that will impose coherence on the text.

Activity also refers to the instructional context in which readers are supported to learn to comprehend and learn from text. There are at least two ways to characterize how students can be taught to comprehend text. One approach is to provide instruction in a set of tools that will support text comprehension activity, and the other is to engage students in conversations in which they collectively participate in constructing the meaning of the text.

The first approach, which is often referred to as *strategy instruction*, has a longer history in the reading literature, whereas the second approach has been garnering more attention recently. In part, this attention is in reaction to the manner in which the first approach has been enacted. Space precludes a full recounting of the history of strategy instruction and why it has foundered, but the gist of the argument is that frequently in the context of strategy instruction, knowledge building with text has been ignored in favor of teaching formal skills that may or may not be used in the service of advancing text comprehension and learning with text (see Duke et al., 2011; Hirsch, 2006; McKeown et al., 2009; Palincsar & Schutz, 2011). The primary goal of a text-based discussion is to support students in understanding the ideas in the text and building knowledge with those ideas. Although processes useful to achieving coherence and building a textbase and situation model of the text may both be modeled and discussed in the course of a text-based discussion, the primary purpose is to collectively construct meaning.

This book was designed to support the use of the second means of comprehension instruction: discussion. We are, of course, not alone in advocating for discussion as the activity context in which to teach comprehension. Wilkinson and Son (2011) provide a comprehensive review of contemporary approaches to reading comprehension instruction that feature discussion.

There are a number of reasons why we focus on discussion. The first is the opportunity that discussion provides for readers to engage in self-explanation. Recall that the ultimate goal of constructing a situation model of the text calls for readers to integrate the new information encountered in the text with their existing knowledge. This integration calls for active construction on the part of the reader. One of the most robust findings in the research literature is the value of engaging learners in explaining the meaning of the text they are reading. Eliciting self-explanations (i.e., asking the reader to explain what a sentence means) has been proven to enhance learning of complex concepts presented in text, whether one compares the amount learned by readers prompted to engage in self-explanation with readers not prompted to do so or compares high versus low explainers. In addition, self-explanation has been documented to promote deeper understanding of content; that is, readers who engaged in self-explanation were able to answer more complex questions regarding the content (Chi, De Leeuw, Chiu, & LaVancher, 1994).

Chi and her colleagues (1994) have argued that self-explaining is a constructive process that encourages the integration of newly acquired information with existing knowledge, supports readers in making the inferences necessary to attain coherence, and gives rise to opportunities for readers to see conflicts between the mental model they are constructing and the description of that model in the text. The lesson plans that we developed for this volume reflect the influence of this literature; we propose discussion moves that engage readers in explaining content, in integrating new content with content previously presented, and in providing evidence for their interpretation of the text so they are comparing the mental representations that they are constructing with one another and with the information in the text.

Whereas the self-explanation literature provides empirical support for the use of text-based discussions, theoretical support is derived from a number of other sources as well. Most prominently, that support comes from sociocultural theory that is represented in the writings of Dewey (1916) and Vygotsky (1978), among others. From a sociocultural perspective, thought, learning, and knowledge are not just influenced by social factors but are, in fact, social phenomena. From this perspective, cognition is a collaborative process (Rogoff, 1998), and thought is internalized discourse; that is, as readers engage in text-based discussions, this experience begins to shape the ways that they approach text even when reading alone (Pontecorvo, 1993).

Research that has been conducted from a sociocultural perspective has been particularly useful for characterizing more and less productive classroom discussion. For example, talk that is interpretive (generated in the service of analysis or explanations) is associated with more significant learning gains than is talk that is simply descriptive, or a retelling of the text (Coleman, 1998). Furthermore, teachers play an important role in mediating classroom discussion by seeding the conversation with new ideas or providing alternative interpretations of the text for students' consideration—moves that are designed to push students' thinking (King, 1990). Finally, these studies speak to the importance of the structure of group activity so responsibility is shared, expertise is distributed, and there is an ethos for building on one another's ideas (Goldenberg, 1992). We return to a discussion of how teachers can influence classroom norms to promote discussion in Chapter 6.

The Sociocultural Context

The final dimension of the RAND Reading Study Group's (2002) model is the sociocultural context in which reader–text–activity interactions take place. Students are, of course, members of many communities beyond the classroom community: families, houses of worship, neighborhoods, language groups, and clubs. Membership in these communities influences the ways in which students have experienced reading and influences the resources students bring to reading.

The contextual issues operate at different levels—classroom, school, community, and indeed national—and can be quite powerful. Neuman and Celano (2001), for example, studied the differential access that parents of young children had to books in Philadelphia neighborhoods that varied significantly in family income. Whereas parents in high-income neighborhoods had their choice of bookstores with well-stocked collections of children's literature, parents in low-income neighborhoods had, at best, convenience stores that carried a paltry selection of choices. Hence, children arrive at school having had significantly different access to literature and different experiences with being read to and talking about stories.

Duke's (2000) study of the availability of informational versus narrative texts in first-grade classrooms of children from well-resourced and poorly resourced communities is another example of how literacy scholars have sought to investigate the role of the sociocultural contexts in which children learn to read. Although children across all communities had few occasions to learn from—or produce—informational text, these occasions were markedly fewer for children in poor communities. The differential access that children have to informational text is one of the most popular explanations for the slump that some students experience as they reach the upper elementary grades and are expected to learn from informational texts.

A number of sociocultural explanations have been tendered for the failure of schools to serve all children; examples include discontinuities between the culture (values, attitudes, and beliefs) of the home and school (Gee, 1990); mismatches in the communicative practices between nonmainstream children and mainstream teachers that lead to miscommunication and misjudgment regarding students (Heath, 1983); the internalization of negative stereotypes by minority groups who have been marginalized and may see school as a site for opposition and resistance (Steele, 1992); and relational issues, such as the failure to attain mutual trust between teachers and students (Moll, 1992) and a shared sense of identification between the teacher and the learner (Cazden, 1993; Litowitz, 1993). These studies provide a mere snapshot of the many reasons why it is important to attend to the sociocultural contexts that shape opportunities that readers have to experience a range of texts, learn to build knowledge with texts, and learn about themselves as readers. In the course of text-based discussions, teachers have opportunities to learn about the resources students are bringing to their reading, to draw on those resources for the good of both the individual and the group, and to build those resources.

Summary

We hope that this chapter has provided useful ways to think about the activity of reading for understanding and knowledge building. We argue that the ultimate goal of comprehension is the building of a situation model in which the reader integrates the ideas presented in the text with prior knowledge that is derived from real-world experiences, as well as from other texts. We believe that a teacher who understands the processes that readers experience in building a situation model is better positioned to guide those processes and to hypothesize what might be impeding readers' sense making with text. Attention to reader factors helps teachers understand the variations in students' engagement and comprehension, while close attention to text features can help teachers (a) make good choices regarding the texts to use for text-based discussion and (b) consider the features of that text that may support students' comprehension or, in fact, impede it. Finally, an awareness that reader–text interactions are influenced by the context in which they take place, as well as the history of reader–text interactions that readers have experienced, can be useful when thinking about the features of the instructional context to which one might aspire. Armed with this specialized knowledge for the teaching of reading comprehension, we now introduce a set of tools designed to support teachers who are striving to prepare classrooms of generous readers.

CHAPTER 2

Planning and Discussing "Harnessing the Wind"

This chapter provides an example of the planning process for a discussion of the text "Harnessing the Wind" by Mason James. The chapter also includes video excerpts showing how a discussion of the text was enacted by Mr. Max Weinberg in a sixth-grade classroom.

Careful Reading of the Text

We begin the planning process with a careful reading of the text, which appears on the following pages. As you read, think about what is most important for students to understand and how you might discuss the text with your students. After an initial reading, return to the text and take some notes. You may want to underline parts of the text or use sticky notes to write comments or mark important parts of the text.

- What are the most important ideas in the text?
- How has the author organized the text to support student understanding of those ideas?
- What are some ideas presented in the text that might pose challenges to students' understanding?
- What text information raises questions in your mind that might be answered by further research?

Harnessing the Wind

BANGOR [ME] DAILY NEWS PHOTO BY BRIDGET BROWN

by Mason James

Vinalhaven is a small island about 15 miles (25 kilometers) off the coast of Maine, and its experience with wind turbines is typical of what happens in many communities. When a power company proposed to build wind turbines on the island, the residents got together to learn about the turbines and vote on the project. Wind turbines are powered by wind, a clean local source of energy that will never run out. They do not require fuel to operate, and they produce no pollution. The people of Vinalhaven liked these aspects of wind power. They also liked being less dependent on their old power plants, which were run by burning coal and diesel fuel. However, some residents expressed their concerns, calling wind turbines dangerous eyesores that would destroy the environment.

Turbine blade being transported through Barton, Vermont

Despite these concerns, support for wind power was overwhelming, and the project moved ahead. Now, the island has three wind turbines with 123-foot-long (37 meters) blades that turn all the time, night and day. As customers of the Fox Island Electric Cooperative, whose rates have gone down, the islanders now pay less for electricity than before. These three turbines generate enough power to cover the needs of the whole island, and then some. Surplus electricity is sold to a power company on the mainland.

But support for the turbines among the islanders is not quite as positive as before. Unfortunately, wind turbines make noise. According to the people of Vinalhaven who live within a half-mile of the turbines, they make a lot of noise—so much that it causes anxiety and stress, and people nearby cannot sleep. Some neighbors say that the noise is no worse than the sound of passing traffic, or the waves on the ocean, or even the noise produced by the old power plant that has since been removed. They just had to get used to the noise, and now they hardly notice it. Animals, such as livestock on farms where wind turbines are installed, tend to do the same. They are disturbed at first by the noise of the turbines, but they soon become accustomed to it and pay no attention.

WIND FARMS

A "wind farm" is a group of wind turbines built in the same place to generate electricity. Wind turbines work best with wind speeds of at least 11 to 13 miles (18 to 22 kilometers) per hour, so wind farms are located in places with strong, steady winds. The best locations are wide open so that large objects such as trees and buildings do not block the wind. Locations that fit these requirements may be on open farmland or prairies, offshore in the ocean or on large lakes, and in mountainous areas along ridgelines. In the United States, the greatest number of wind farms are located in the central plains states, from North Dakota to Texas, and along the West Coast. The Northeast has a smaller number of wind farms, especially in Maine and New York, but the Southeast has very few.

Harnessing the Wind | **2**

HISTORY OF WIND POWER

People have used wind power for thousands of years, beginning with sailboats that used wind power for transportation. From there, people built sail-powered windmills on land to take advantage of wind power for other uses. The first windmills were built in Persia more than 1,200 years ago to pump water out of the ground. Next, windmills were built for grinding grain. The power of the wind was harnessed by wooden blades, or sails, and used to turn large, heavy grinding stones. Later, windmills were used for other tasks, such as irrigating farmlands and processing lumber. Using wind power was much easier than trying to accomplish these tasks by hand.

120 - 176 feet (36 - 54 m)

300 feet (91 m)

Some people on Vinalhaven object to the wind turbines for other reasons. One reason is visual. Some people think that the turbines are ugly and that they spoil the beautiful scenery of the island. Other people are more concerned about wildlife and the environment. They believe that wind turbines kill large numbers of birds and bats, and the loss of these flying creatures upsets the natural balance of the ecosystem. Experts have studied this problem in great detail. Many scientists agree that wind turbines may cause the death of as many as 10 birds per year for each turbine. The number of birds killed by the turbines on Vinalhaven is much less than that.

How Wind Turbines Work

Wind is a movement of air caused by differences in air pressure, heating and cooling, and the rotation of the earth. As the air around the earth is warmed by the sun, it expands and becomes less dense, and the air pressure decreases. Warm air tends to rise. Cooler air is heavier and has more pressure. When warm air rises, cooler air rushes in to take its place. We experience this process as wind blowing, and this wind has a lot of energy.

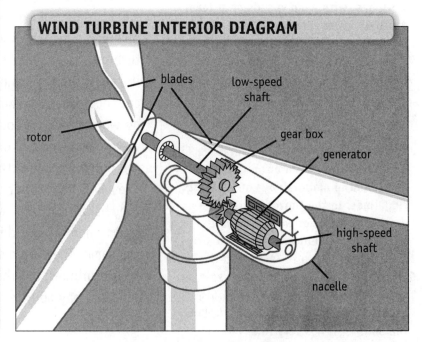

WIND TURBINE INTERIOR DIAGRAM

blades

low-speed shaft

rotor

gear box

generator

high-speed shaft

nacelle

Harnessing the Wind | 3

Wind turbines take the kinetic energy of the wind and turn it into mechanical power. This mechanical power can be used for work such as grinding grain in a gristmill or pumping water out of the ground, or it can be converted into electricity. When the wind blows, the wind turns the blades of the turbine. The movement of the blades turns a shaft, which is connected to a generator. The generator uses the mechanical power of the turning shaft to produce electricity.

Depending on their size, wind turbines can produce a few hundred kilowatts of electricity per hour—enough to power a few homes. A group of wind turbines, called a wind farm, can produce several megawatts of electricity per hour. That is enough to power a small town, such as Vinalhaven.

The Future of Wind Power

Until recently, wind power was most common in Europe, and Germany produced more wind power than any other country. But in 2009, the United States overtook Germany as the world's largest producer. Experts at the U.S. Department of Energy believe that wind power can provide for 20 percent of our nation's electricity by 2030.

Other nations, such as China, are developing wind power even faster than the United States. China became the world's largest producer in 2010. Before long, there will be wind turbines in practically every part of the world.

TOP TEN PRODUCERS OF WIND POWER (2010)

Country	Production Capacity (MW)
China	41,800
United States	40,200
Germany	27,214
Spain	20,676
India	13,065
Italy	5,797
France	5,660
United Kingdom	5,204
Canada	4,008
Denmark	3,752

Harnessing the Wind | 4

Reading the Text: Our Notes

Here are the notes that we made while reading "Harnessing the Wind." Compare your notations with ours.

Text	Our Notes
page 1	
Harnessing the Wind by Mason James Vinalhaven is a small island about 15 miles (25 kilometers) off the coast of Maine, and its experience with wind turbines is typical of what happens in many communities. When a power company proposed to build wind turbines on the island, the residents got together to learn about the turbines and vote on the project. Wind turbines are powered by wind, a clean local source of energy that will never run out. They do not require fuel to operate, and they produce no pollution. The people of Vinalhaven liked these aspects of wind power. They also liked being less dependent on their old power plants, which were run by burning coal and diesel fuel. However, some residents expressed their concerns, calling wind turbines dangerous eyesores that would destroy the environment.	• This first paragraph sets up the idea that there are many positive aspects of using wind turbines: use clean, local energy source (wind), need no fuel, do not pollute. • The paragraph also contrasts wind power to power produced in power plants that burn coal and diesel fuel. • *However* is an important word here. Some residents were concerned about the wind turbines being eyesores in the landscape and also destroying the environment. • So there are also negative aspects of using wind turbines. • An eyesore is something that is unpleasant to see. • The citizens learned about wind turbines, and after gathering information, they voted.
page 2	
Despite these concerns, support for wind power was overwhelming, and the project moved ahead. Now, the island has three wind turbines with 123-foot-long (37 meters) blades that turn all the time, night and day. As customers of the Fox Island Electric Cooperative, whose rates have gone down, the islanders now pay less for electricity than before. These three turbines generate enough power to cover the needs of the whole island, and then some. Surplus electricity is sold to a power company on the mainland.	• Despite concerns (mentioned on p. 1), the project (building the wind turbines) moved ahead. *Despite* is important cue. • To get a sense of the size of the wind turbine blades (123 ft/37 m), use pickup truck as reference point in photo and measure how many pickup trucks could be placed side by side to show how long one blade is. • Connect with concerns and eyesore. • More positive effects of wind turbines: lower electric bills, surplus electricity can be sold *(continued)*

Text	Our Notes
page 2 *continued*	
But support for the turbines among the islanders is not quite as positive as before. Unfortunately, wind turbines make noise. According to the people of Vinalhaven who live within a half-mile of the turbines, they make a lot of noise—so much that it causes anxiety and stress, and people nearby cannot sleep. Some neighbors say that the noise is no worse than the sound of passing traffic, or the waves on the ocean, or even the noise produced by the old power plant that has since been removed. They just had to get used to the noise, and now they hardly notice it. Animals, such as livestock on farms where wind turbines are installed, tend to do the same. They are disturbed at first by the noise of the turbines, but they soon become accustomed to it and pay no attention.	• *But* is an important word. • Wind turbines cause noise. • People say they can't sleep. • Others say that the noise is no worse than what the old power plant produced. • Animals get used to the noise.
page 2 sidebar	
Wind Farms A "wind farm" is a group of wind turbines built in the same place to generate electricity. Wind turbines work best with wind speeds of at least 11 to 13 miles (18 to 22 kilometers) per hour, so wind farms are located in places with strong, steady winds. The best locations are wide open so that large objects such as trees and buildings do not block the wind. Locations that fit these requirements may be on open farmland or prairies, offshore in the ocean or on large lakes, and in mountainous areas along ridgelines. In the United States, the greatest number of wind farms are located in the central plains states, from North Dakota to Texas, and along the West Coast. The Northeast has a smaller number of wind farms, especially in Maine and New York, but the Southeast has very few.	• Information about where wind farms are built.
page 3	
Some people on Vinalhaven object to the wind turbines for other reasons. One reason is visual. Some people think that the turbines are ugly and that they spoil the beautiful scenery of the island. Other people are more concerned about wildlife and the environment. They believe that wind turbines kill large numbers of birds and bats, and the loss of these flying creatures upsets the natural balance of the ecosystem. Experts have studied this problem in great detail. Many scientists agree that wind turbines may cause the death of as many as 10 birds per year for each turbine. The number of birds killed by the turbines on Vinalhaven is much less than that.	• The presentation of positive and negative aspects of wind turbines continues. • Negative: Wind turbines are ugly (eyesores, p. 1), and they kill birds and upset ecosystem balance. • Positive: Fewer than 10 birds are killed by each wind turbine on Vinalhaven. *(continued)*

Text	Our Notes
page 3	
How Wind Turbines Work Wind is a movement of air caused by differences in air pressure, heating and cooling, and the rotation of the earth. As the air around the earth is warmed by the sun, it expands and becomes less dense, and the air pressure decreases. Warm air tends to rise. Cooler air is heavier and has more pressure. When warm air rises, cooler air rushes in to take its place. We experience this process as wind blowing, and this wind has a lot of energy.	• This heading signals that the text is going to focus on a different aspect of wind turbines: how they work. • This paragraph provides a very general explanation of what causes wind. • Energy = capacity to do work
page 3 sidebar	
History of Wind Power People have used wind power for thousands of years, beginning with sailboats that used wind power for transportation. From there, people built sail-powered windmills on land to take advantage of wind power for other uses. The first windmills were built in Persia more than 1,200 years ago to pump water out of the ground. Next, windmills were built for grinding grain. The power of the wind was harnessed by wooden blades, or sails, and used to turn large, heavy grinding stones. Later, windmills were used for other tasks, such as irrigating farmlands and processing lumber. Using wind power was much easier than trying to accomplish these tasks by hand.	• The information in this sidebar explains the kind of work that wind can do.
page 4	
Wind turbines take the kinetic energy of the wind and turn it into mechanical power. This mechanical power can be used for work such as grinding grain in a gristmill or pumping water out of the ground, or it can be converted into electricity. When the wind blows, the wind turns the blades of the turbine. The movement of the blades turns a shaft, which is connected to a generator. The generator uses the mechanical power of the turning shaft to produce electricity.	• The information in this paragraph refers to the diagram on p. 3. • A nacelle (nuh-SEL) is a covering over working parts in a machine. • Kinetic energy refers to energy created by movement. In this case, the movement of the wind turbine blades. • The energy conversion that takes place when a wind turbine is used to generate electricity is quite complicated. • This explanation is very general.
Depending on their size, wind turbines can produce a few hundred kilowatts of electricity per hour—enough to power a few homes. A group of wind turbines, called a wind farm, can produce several megawatts of electricity per hour. That is enough to power a small town, such as Vinalhaven.	• Wind farms are explained here. *(continued)*

Text	Our Notes
page 4 *continued*	
The Future of Wind Power Until recently, wind power was most common in Europe, and Germany produced more wind power than any other country. But in 2009, the United States overtook Germany as the world's largest producer. Experts at the U.S. Department of Energy believe that wind power can provide for 20 percent of our nation's electricity by 2030. Other nations, such as China, are developing wind power even faster than the United States. China became the world's largest producer in 2010. Before long, there will be wind turbines in practically every part of the world.	• This last section provides information about international wind power production. • The author makes the claim that there will soon be wind turbines "in practically every part of the world."

Analyzing the Text

After reading, we review our notes and analyze the text in terms of:

- **Content**
  - What is the important content presented in the text?
  - How can that information be organized to create a coherent mental representation?
  - What conceptual challenges does the text present? What concepts might be difficult to understand?

- **Research**
  - What additional information do I need to feel confident in teaching with this text?
  - What topics might students want to know more about?

- **Text features**
  - How is information communicated in the text? What is the overall organization of text information? Do the paragraphs include topic sentences?
  - What language cues does the author use to support coherence building? For example, does the author use connectives to relate or compare information? Are there supportive transitions between paragraphs?
  - What graphic features does the text provide?

- **Disciplinary knowledge**
  - What information in the text relates to how knowledge is generated, presented, and critiqued in a specific domain?
  - What can students learn about the work of disciplinary experts?

These ways of thinking about a text are interrelated. However, we have found it helpful to analyze a text by considering each of these perspectives in turn.

Analyzing "Harnessing the Wind"

We analyzed "Harnessing the Wind" by focusing on important content, useful text features, and opportunities to develop disciplinary knowledge.

Content

"Harnessing the Wind" provides information about what wind turbines do: create electricity through the power of the wind. Although the article includes information about how wind turbines work and the international use of wind power, that information is very general and superficial. The text doesn't really lend itself to an in-depth consideration of the physics involved in transforming wind energy into electrical energy.

We see the most important information in the text as the description of the pros and cons of using wind turbines and how citizens had to weigh those pros and cons to make a decision.

Research

We sometimes find it necessary to do some research to support our own understanding of text information. When we researched wind turbines, we discovered that the process of converting wind power to electricity is quite complicated. We agreed that the focus of the article was not on that topic but rather on the pros and cons of wind turbines.

We wondered how predictable the output of wind turbines was. Our research revealed that if a wind turbine is located in an optimal location, the total output is relatively stable across years. There can be variability, however, across seasons and times of day.

We looked up the meaning and pronunciation of the term *nacelle*, which appears in the diagram on page 3.

Text Features

The text provides opportunities for focusing on language cues, graphics, and sidebars as special text features.

- *Language cues:* The author uses the contrastive connectives *however*, *but*, and *despite* to connect contrasting viewpoints and features related to the use of wind turbines. The author uses key referents to refer to the building of the wind turbines (project) and to the ideas that wind turbines are eyesores and dangers to the environment (concerns).

- *Graphics:* The photographs on pages 1, 2, and 3 of the article can be used to get a sense of how big wind turbine blades are and how their size relates to concerns about their impact on the landscape and environment. The diagram on page 3 is a simplified illustration of the internal parts of a wind turbine.

- *Sidebars:* The sidebar on page 2 provides important information about the features of locations chosen for wind farms. The sidebar on page 3 provides information that explains how wind can do work.

Disciplinary Knowledge

"Harnessing the Wind" does not offer opportunities for students to learn about the work of experts such as historians, scientists, or archaeologists. Such opportunities are provided in other texts that we will consider. However, the article does provide an opportunity for students to think about civic literacy, the knowledge and skills needed for effective participation in a community.

Selecting Learning Goals

Every discussion plan that we design begins with the learning goals. The goals represent aspects of the coherent mental representation that students will be supported to construct through the discussion. The goals are the destination, and the discussion plan is the road map.

The goals can be shared with students as part of the introduction to the text, which we refer to as the discussion launch. You will see Mr. Weinberg doing this in the video episodes later in this chapter. Displaying the goals on chart paper provides a focus for the discussion and a reference point. After the discussion, the goals can be referred to as a way to summarize what was learned through the discussion.

When we develop learning goals for a discussion about a specific text, we consider the same three perspectives that guided our analysis of the text: content, text features, and disciplinary knowledge.

Here are the learning goals that we selected for "Harnessing the Wind":

1. What are wind turbines used for?

   Wind turbines are used to create electricity from the movement of wind.

2. What were the pros and cons of wind turbines that citizens of Vinalhaven considered as they decided whether to build them on their island home?

Pros	Cons
• Clean source of energy (no pollution) • Efficient (can produce surplus energy) • Can lower electric bills	• Noisy (but people and animals could get used to the noise) • Eyesores • Harm birds and ecosystem

3. What language cues do authors use to connect ideas in a text?

   Authors can use referents to refer to an idea, object, or event in more than one way.

   Authors can use contrastive connectives such as *however*, *despite*, and *but* to contrast ideas, opinions, or features.

4. How can photographs provide clues to the size of objects described in a text?

   Objects in a photograph can be used as a point of reference for measuring the size of an object.

   Consulting more than one photograph can provide supporting evidence for a measurement.

The first learning goal describes an obvious knowledge-building outcome of reading about wind turbines. The second—thinking about pros and cons—provides a way for students to organize the information in the article, to impose coherence on the text information. The third—paying attention to language cues—develops students' knowledge of how texts work and how specific language cues can help them understand text information. In meeting the fourth learning goal, students will learn how to make use of visual cues to answer questions they may have.

Designing the Exit

Given the learning goals, we next think about the exit, or end, of the discussion. Picking up on the analogy of the discussion plan as a road map, how will you know if students have reached the destination? To answer that question, we design an exit activity that engages students after the discussion.

At the conclusion of Mr. Weinberg's discussion, he asked students to vote on the question below. We thought it was a good idea to have students work in small groups to talk about the question first and then vote. Our suggested exit would include a prompt such as the following:

Based on what you have learned about wind turbines, would you vote to have a wind turbine built nearby to power our school? Read the information in the sidebar on page 2 before you make your decision.

After the discussion, we would have students vote by secret ballot to indicate their choice and their main reason for making that choice. We would also display student responses in a graph or table or ask volunteers to do so.

Designing the Launch

Once we have decided on the learning goals and exit, we consider how we will launch the discussion. The launch is the beginning of students' journey toward the learning goals.

We admired Mr. Weinberg's launch, which you will see later in this chapter, and decided to use it with just a few modifications for ours:

- Elicit students' prior knowledge about, or experiences with, wind turbines.
- Establish meaning of the key word *harness* in the title.
- Post questions (learning goals) to guide student thinking about text.

Designing the Discussion Plan

Once we have decided on the learning goals, exit, and launch, we plan the road map that will support students on their journey through the text. Part of the road map includes how the text will be read. Knowing your students, you can decide whether you will read parts or all of the text, or ask students to read. Planning also involves deciding how much students will read before you ask them to stop and talk about what they are learning. Deciding when and where to stop is a critical feature of planning for a discussion. Stopping too often or reading too much can interfere with students' development of mental representations of text information. The purpose for stopping has to be to focus student attention on important ideas. Those ideas can be presented in one sentence, a few sentences, or several paragraphs. What you ask students to do at each stopping point is also a critical feature of the discussion plan, or road map. We use the term *reader–text interactions* to refer to the questions, prompts, and activities that we engage students in at each stopping point.

In the section that follows, we show how our analysis of "Harnessing the Wind" and the learning goals that we selected informed the design of a discussion plan for reading and talking about the text. The words in *italics* are what we would say to students. We offer our discussion plan not as a script but rather as one way to guide students in comprehending the text, organizing text ideas into a coherent mental representation.

Discussion Plan for "Harnessing the Wind"

Learning Goals

1. What are wind turbines used for?

   Wind turbines are used to create electricity from the movement of wind.

2. What were the pros and cons of wind turbines that citizens of Vinalhaven considered as they decided whether to build them on their island home?

Pros	Cons
• Clean source of energy (no pollution) • Efficient (can produce surplus energy) • Can lower electric bills	• Noisy (but people and animals could get used to the noise) • Eyesores • Harm birds and ecosystem

3. What language cues do authors use to connect ideas in a text?

   Authors can use referents to refer to an idea, object, or event in more than one way.

   Authors can use contrastive connectives such as *however*, *despite*, and *but* to contrast ideas, opinions, or features.

4. How can photographs provide clues to the size of objects described in a text?

   Objects in a photograph can be used as a point of reference for measuring the size of an object.

   Consulting more than one photograph can provide supporting evidence for a measurement.

Resources

- Copies of "Harnessing the Wind"
- Chart paper with the following questions:
    1. What are wind turbines used for?
    2. What were the pros and cons of wind turbines that citizens of Vinalhaven considered as they decided whether to build them on their island home?
    3. What language cues do authors use to connect ideas in a text?
    4. How can photographs provide clues to the size of objects described in a text?

- Chart paper with the following heading and columns:

Building Wind Turbines on Vinalhaven

Pros	Cons

- Rulers
- Ballots for students to use in voting for or against building wind turbines to power their school

Launch

Distribute copies of the article "Harnessing the Wind."

The photograph on this page shows wind turbines. What do you already know about wind turbines?

The title of this article is "Harnessing the Wind." When you read the word harnessing, *you might think about a horse because a harness is used to control the movements of a horse. But you can harness, or control, other things. In this article, we will read about how people are trying to control and use the power of the wind. This is a nonfiction or informational article. We can expect to learn something about wind turbines by reading and talking about it.*

I've posted some questions here on this chart paper.

1. *What are wind turbines used for?*

2. *What were the pros and cons of wind turbines that citizens of Vinalhaven considered as they decided whether to build them on their island home? (The term* pros *means positive features or reasons to support something. The term* cons *means negative features or reasons to not support something.)*

3. *What language cues do authors use to connect ideas in a text?*

4. *How can photographs provide clues to the size of objects described in a text?*

These questions should guide our thinking as we read "Harnessing the Wind." After reading, you should be able to answer these questions.

Let's get started.

The **bolded** text in the following table provides instructions for what you should do. Instructions to read, for example, mean that you or a volunteer should read the indicated text aloud.

Text	Our Notes	Reader–Text Interactions
page 1		
Harnessing the Wind by Mason James Vinalhaven is a small island about 15 miles (25 kilometers) off the coast of Maine, and its experience with wind turbines is typical of what happens in many communities. When a power company proposed to build wind turbines on the island, the residents got together to learn about the turbines and vote on the project. Wind turbines are powered by wind, a clean local source of energy that will never run out. They do not require fuel to operate, and they produce no pollution. The people of Vinalhaven liked these aspects of wind power. They also liked being less dependent on their old power plants, which were run by burning coal and diesel fuel. However, some residents expressed their concerns, calling wind turbines dangerous eyesores that would destroy the environment.	• This first paragraph sets up the idea that there are many positive aspects of using wind turbines: use clean, local energy source (wind), need no fuel, do not pollute. • The paragraph also contrasts wind power to power produced in power plants that burn coal and diesel fuel. • *However* is an important word here. Some residents were concerned about the wind turbines being eyesores in the landscape and also destroying the environment. • So there are also negative aspects of using wind turbines. • An eyesore is something that is unpleasant to see. • The citizens learned about wind turbines, and after gathering information, they voted.	• **Read the title and the first paragraph.** • *So the people on this little island were approached by a power company about building wind turbines. What did they like about the idea, or what were some pros for building the wind turbines?* • *Notice that the last sentence begins with the word* however. *However is a language cue. It cues readers to expect a contrast or difference. We've been reading about the pros of building turbines. The word* however *cues us to expect some cons. What are the cons that some residents had about the wind turbines?* • *What are eyesores?* • *After considering the pros and cons of wind turbines, what did the citizens of Vinalhaven do?* • *It's important to note that their vote came after their information gathering. They were informed voters.* *(continued)*

Text	Our Notes	Reader–Text Interactions
page 2		
Despite these concerns, support for wind power was overwhelming, and the project moved ahead. Now, the island has three wind turbines with 123-foot-long (37 meters) blades that turn all the time, night and day. As customers of the Fox Island Electric Cooperative, whose rates have gone down, the islanders now pay less for electricity than before. These three turbines generate enough power to cover the needs of the whole island, and then some. Surplus electricity is sold to a power company on the mainland.	• Despite concerns (mentioned on p. 1), the project (building the wind turbines) moved ahead. *Despite* is important cue. • To get a sense of the size of the wind turbine blades (123 ft/37 m), use pickup truck as reference point in photo and measure how many pickup trucks could be placed side by side to show how long one blade is. • Connect with concerns and eyesore. • More positive effects of wind turbines: lower electric bills, surplus electricity can be sold	• **Read the first two sentences.** • *Let's stop right there. Here's another language cue: the word* despite. *What's another way of saying "Despite these concerns"?* • *What does the word* concerns *refer to? Why might the wind turbines be called eyesores?* • *Let's use the photograph on this page to figure out just how big one wind turbine blade is. How might we do that?* • *One way is to use the pickup truck as a reference point. Use a sheet of paper or ruler to measure the pickup truck. (about an inch) How many pickup trucks long is the wind turbine blade? (about 6½)* • *Look at the diagram on page 3 in the sidebar. So, about how long is a wind turbine blade?* • **Read the rest of the paragraph.** • *So, what pros, or positive effects, of wind turbines did we learn about?* • *Let's start writing some of this information about the pros and cons of wind turbines on this table.* *(continued)*

Text	Our Notes	Reader–Text Interactions
page 2 continued		
But support for the turbines among the islanders is not quite as positive as before. Unfortunately, wind turbines make noise. According to the people of Vinalhaven who live within a half-mile of the turbines, they make a lot of noise—so much that it causes anxiety and stress, and people nearby cannot sleep. Some neighbors say that the noise is no worse than the sound of passing traffic, or the waves on the ocean, or even the noise produced by the old power plant that has since been removed. They just had to get used to the noise, and now they hardly notice it. Animals, such as livestock on farms where wind turbines are installed, tend to do the same. They are disturbed at first by the noise of the turbines, but they soon become accustomed to it and pay no attention.	• *But* is an important word. • Wind turbines cause noise. • People say they can't sleep. • Others say that the noise is no worse than what the old power plant produced. • Animals get used to the noise.	• **Read the next paragraph.** • **Invite students to add to the Pros and Cons table.**
page 2 sidebar		
Wind Farms A "wind farm" is a group of wind turbines built in the same place to generate electricity. Wind turbines work best with wind speeds of at least 11 to 13 miles (18 to 22 kilometers) per hour, so wind farms are located in places with strong, steady winds. The best locations are wide open so that large objects such as trees and buildings do not block the wind. Locations that fit these requirements may be on open farmland or prairies, offshore in the ocean or on large lakes, and in mountainous areas along ridgelines. In the United States, the greatest number of wind farms are located in the central plains states, from North Dakota to Texas, and along the West Coast. The Northeast has a smaller number of wind farms, especially in Maine and New York, but the Southeast has very few.	• Information about where wind farms are built.	• *You will have a chance to read the sidebar on this page later. Move on to page 3.* *(continued)*

Text	Our Notes	Reader–Text Interactions
page 3		
Some people on Vinalhaven object to the wind turbines for other reasons. One reason is visual. Some people think that the turbines are ugly and that they spoil the beautiful scenery of the island. Other people are more concerned about wildlife and the environment. They believe that wind turbines kill large numbers of birds and bats, and the loss of these flying creatures upsets the natural balance of the ecosystem. Experts have studied this problem in great detail. Many scientists agree that wind turbines may cause the death of as many as 10 birds per year for each turbine. The number of birds killed by the turbines on Vinalhaven is much less than that.	• The presentation of positive and negative aspects of wind turbines continues. • Negative: Wind turbines are ugly (eyesores, p. 1), and they kill birds and upset ecosystem balance. • Positive: Fewer than 10 birds are killed by each wind turbine on Vinalhaven.	• **Read the paragraph.** • **Invite students to add more items to the Pros and Cons table.**
How Wind Turbines Work Wind is a movement of air caused by differences in air pressure, heating and cooling, and the rotation of the earth. As the air around the earth is warmed by the sun, it expands and becomes less dense, and the air pressure decreases. Warm air tends to rise. Cooler air is heavier and has more pressure. When warm air rises, cooler air rushes in to take its place. We experience this process as wind blowing, and this wind has a lot of energy.	• This heading signals that the text is going to focus on a different aspect of wind turbines: how they work. • This paragraph provides a very general explanation of what causes wind. • Energy = capacity to do work	• **Read the heading.** • *This heading signals that the author is going to introduce a new topic. We've been reading about the pros and cons of wind turbines. Now we will read about how wind turbines work.* • **Read the paragraph.** • *Wind is something that we might take for granted, but it is a very complex phenomenon, or occurrence. The important idea here is that air moves because of changes in temperature and pressure.* • *Another important idea in this paragraph is that wind has energy. Scientists describe energy as the capacity to do work.* (continued)

Text	Our Notes	Reader–Text Interactions
page 3 sidebar		
History of Wind Power People have used wind power for thousands of years, beginning with sailboats that used wind power for transportation. From there, people built sail-powered windmills on land to take advantage of wind power for other uses. The first windmills were built in Persia more than 1,200 years ago to pump water out of the ground. Next, windmills were built for grinding grain. The power of the wind was harnessed by wooden blades, or sails, and used to turn large, heavy grinding stones. Later, windmills were used for other tasks, such as irrigating farmlands and processing lumber. Using wind power was much easier than trying to accomplish these tasks by hand.	• The information in this sidebar explains the kind of work that wind can do.	• *The sidebar on this page describes the kind of work that wind can do.* • **Read the sidebar.**
page 4		
Wind turbines take the kinetic energy of the wind and turn it into mechanical power. This mechanical power can be used for work such as grinding grain in a gristmill or pumping water out of the ground, or it can be converted into electricity. When the wind blows, the wind turns the blades of the turbine. The movement of the blades turns a shaft, which is connected to a generator. The generator uses the mechanical power of the turning shaft to produce electricity.	• The information in this paragraph refers to the diagram on p. 3. • A nacelle (nuh-SEL) is a covering over working parts in a machine. • Kinetic energy refers to energy created by movement. In this case, the movement of the wind turbine blades. • The energy conversion that takes place when a wind turbine is used to generate electricity is quite complicated. • This explanation is very general.	• **Read the first two sentences.** • *The author explains that kinetic energy is energy that comes from things that move, so the movement of the wind is what he is referring to here.* • *Turn back to page 3 and look at the diagram at the bottom of that page while I read the next sentences.* • **Read the rest of the paragraph.** • *There's more to the wind turbine than what is shown here. Other important parts generate electricity and transport it.*
Depending on their size, wind turbines can produce a few hundred kilowatts of electricity per hour—enough to power a few homes. A group of wind turbines, called a wind farm, can produce several megawatts of electricity per hour. That is enough to power a small town, such as Vinalhaven.	• Wind farms are explained here.	• **Continue reading.** *(continued)*

Text	Our Notes	Reader–Text Interactions
page 4 continued		
The Future of Wind Power Until recently, wind power was most common in Europe, and Germany produced more wind power than any other country. But in 2009, the United States overtook Germany as the world's largest producer. Experts at the U.S. Department of Energy believe that wind power can provide for 20 percent of our nation's electricity by 2030. Other nations, such as China, are developing wind power even faster than the United States. China became the world's largest producer in 2010. Before long, there will be wind turbines in practically every part of the world.	• This last section provides information about international wind power production. • The author makes the claim that there will soon be wind turbines "in practically every part of the world."	• **Read the heading.** • This heading signals a new topic: the future of wind power. • **Read the paragraphs.** • *What does this last sentence mean: "Before long, there will be wind turbines in practically every part of the world"?* • *How does the sentence connect to what we've been writing about the pros and cons of wind turbines?*

Exit

Before joining your small group, read the sidebar entitled "Wind Farms" on page 2. This is new information that you can use to inform your thinking about wind turbines. Then, in your small groups, talk about what you've learned about the pros and cons of wind turbines. Based on what you've learned, would you vote to have a wind turbine built nearby to power our school?

After the discussion, invite students to vote by secret ballot to indicate their choice and write in their main reason for making that choice.

For wind turbines _____   Against wind turbines _____

Main reason for your choice:

Count the votes for and against wind turbines and have a student mark those on chart paper or the board. You may also want to list the most common reasons given in support or opposition.

Some Important Moves in the Discussion Plan

Here we describe some of the discussion moves that we used in the discussion plan for "Harnessing the Wind."

- *Making it real:* Using the photograph to measure the size of the wind turbine blade can be a memorable experience for students, one that they may remember and try themselves when they are reading other texts on their own.

- *Supplying information:* Notice how we handled the text about how wind turbines work. Because it is so general, we supplied the important information, cueing students by saying, "The important idea here is…." We used this same move with the next paragraph in the same section, "There's more to wind turbines than what is shown here…."

- *Focusing on specific phrases and sentences:* We used this move when we asked students to provide another way of saying "Despite these concerns" and again at the end of the discussion when we focused student attention on the sentence "Before long, there will be wind turbines in practically every part of the world."

Viewing Video Episodes

The video episodes for this chapter feature Mr. Weinberg and a group of sixth graders discussing "Harnessing the Wind." He reads the text aloud, making it accessible to all students. Asking students to volunteer to read is another option, but Mr. Weinberg was working with a group of students whom he was meeting for the first time.

Video Episode 2.1: Launching the Discussion

Let's start with the launch, or how a text is introduced and students are prepared to think about text ideas. We noticed that Mr. Weinberg used a sequence of three discussion moves in his launch. See what you notice as you watch the video episode noted below. Jot down your ideas and then compare them with our notes in the table below.

 2.1: Launching the Discussion (4:11)

Video Episode 2.1: Launching the Discussion	Our Notes
Mr. W: OK? Let's get started. Everyone, look at this text. It's called "Harnessing the Wind." And the images on here—or the image, this is a photograph—it shows a big piece of land with some wind turbines. Does everyone see the wind turbines? Does anyone know what wind turbines are? Go ahead, Precious. Precious: It is like solar-powered windmills or something? [twirling her fingers]	• Mr. Weinberg directs students to the photograph. • He identifies the wind turbines. • He elicits students' prior knowledge about wind turbines. *(continued)*

Video Episode 2.1: Launching the Discussion *continued*	Our Notes
Mr. W: Windmill—yeah, well they look like windmills, right? They're solar-powered windmills. So there's something about solar power or energy, and they go like this. [makes circles with finger] Do that again. That's important. This is what they do. Go ahead.	• He picks up Precious's language about "solar-powered windmills" but restates, or revoices, her contribution as "energy." • He marks the importance of Precious's hand movements.
Student: It provides electricity only when the wind is blowing.	
Mr. W: Oh, you know some stuff. So they provide—the wind does what?	• He continues to elicit student contributions and shares his own experiences.
Student: It spins the, the, whatever it's called.	
Mr. W: Spins the fan or whatever that is.	
Student: And the long—like it can, it can start the electricity, but when it's at night and there's no wind, it stops.	
Mr. W: Good. So I'm from Chicago, which is in Illinois, and there are some wind turbines, especially like in southern Illinois. So I've seen them before, and I've seen them when I've been driving the other w—to Wisconsin—in Wisconsin.	
Mr. W: You're all experts at Michigan. Have you ever seen wind turbines around Michigan, around here? Raise your hand if you've seen some in person. Maybe? OK. Let's start—let's look at the title again for a second: "Harnessing the Wind." Does anyone know what a harness is? The first word says *harnessing*. Does anyone know what a harness is? You know? Cody, what do you think?	• He directs attention to the title of the article. • He elicits students' understanding of the keyword *harness*.
Cody: It's something that you wear, and it's like something that you would wear if you went mountain climbing or something like that to keep you from falling.	
Mr. W: Great! So a mountain climber might strap it on or a hiker might strap it on if they're going into a dangerous, risky situation. And what does it do?	• He connects student contribution of mountain-climbing harness to horse harness and then to idea that harness controls the wind.
Student: It protects you from like falling a certain distance.	
Mr. W: Good. Like you might go a little bit, but then it'll pull you back. And if—you may have seen images of someone riding a horse or making a horse go, and they would have a har— The horse has a harness attached to them, and someone uses the reins on the horse, and it pulls the harness so that the horse— You can control the horse a little bit. So harnessing the wind is about the work that this machine does. It kind of collects the wind. You hold on to the wind to do something with it.	

(continued)

Video Episode 2.1: Launching the Discussion *continued*	Our Notes
Mr. W: And we're gonna read to find out what that something is. We're gon—as we're talking today, these are three questions I want to make sure that you think about and that when you walk out of here, you feel like you can talk about, even teach maybe younger students or other sixth graders about. [pointing to chart paper with three questions] The first thing is, What are wind turbines for? And there are already some ideas floating around in the room, I think. Next, what are the arguments for wind turbines? Like why might someone, even in your community, really want a wind turbine here? And then, what are the arguments against wind turbines? So you can see here I underlined *for*, and here I mean *against*.	• He posts questions to guide thinking about text.
Mr. W: These are opposites, right? Why would someone not want a wind turbine? Do you already have an idea, Jasmine?	
Jasmine: Yeah, I got one for the second one. The reason why people would say they would want wind turbines is because they, they like—they're—they help, and they're, they're not like using electricity, but they're just by the wind. They're using the wind and the energy instead of electricity powering it.	
Mr. W: Interesting. Have you read this already?	
Jasmine: No.	
Mr. W: You just know a lot. That's great. OK, let's see if we can find evidence of what Jasmine's talking about in this article 'cause that makes a lot of sense. That would be a good reason to be, you were saying, *for* it. OK?	• In about four minutes, he has prepared students to begin reading and thinking about the text.

Video Episode 2.2: Returning to the Text

Let's look at another video episode. We selected this episode because Mr. Weinberg uses an important discussion move. Again, jot down what you notice and then compare your notes with ours.

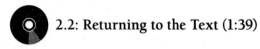 2.2: Returning to the Text (1:39)

Video Episode 2.2: Returning to the Text	Our Notes
Mr. W: This school has solar panels. That's awesome. So this school might actually be getting energy from a natural source like the sun. Did anyone hear anything about power plants? Because other places besides this school aren't—I don't see so many solar, solar panels in other places. Look back at the paragraph on the first page. If you already went to page 1—I mean, if you already went to page 2, go back to page 1, everybody. Find these two words. It's toward the bottom of the page. Find the words *power plants* and put that finger on those two words. They're right next to each other. Jerome, you found 'em?	
Jerome: Mm-hmm.	
Mr. W: OK. Can you back up to the beginning of that sentence?	• Mr. Weinberg uses the discussion move of having students return to the text. He does this to make sure they understand the important idea that wind power is an alternative to power plants that burn coal and diesel fuel.
Jerome [reading]: "They also liked being less dependent on their old power plants, which were being—were, were run by burning coal and diesel fuel."	
Mr. W: Diesel fuel, great. Does it sound like coal and diesel fuel are natural and really healthy for us?	
Student: No.	
Mr. W: No. OK, I want us to really understand that, that coal and diesel fuel and all the work that has to go into getting those things ready to even make energy take a lot of work, a lot of energy, and add pollution to the world. OK? I want to make sure we understand that, that, that that's very different than wind turbines. OK?	• He links power plants and pollution so students understand the connection and how that differs from the energy supplied by wind turbines.

Video Episodes 2.3.1: Language Cues and 2.3.2: "Turn and Talk"

This time we invite you to look at two video episodes. We selected these because Mr. Weinberg uses several important discussion moves. Again, jot down what you notice and then compare your notes with ours.

 2.3.1: Language Cues (1:14)

Video Episode 2.3.1: Language Cues	Our Notes
Mr. W: Top of page 2, I'm gonna start reading. [reading] "Despite these concerns, support for wind power was overwhelming, and the project moved ahead." What's the project we're talking about? Octavius, what's the project we're talking about? Octavius: The project about wind turbines? Mr. W: About whether to put wind turbines on this island or not, right? Octavius: Yes.	• Mr. Weinberg makes sure that students understand what the referent *project* refers to (building wind turbines).
Mr. W: So there were some concerns, but it's going ahead. What were the concerns? Jasmine, do you remember what the concerns were? Jasmine: Support for wind power was overwhelming and [inaudible].	• He also makes sure that students understand what the referent *concerns* refers to (that the huge wind turbines are eyesores).
Mr. W: Well that's, that's— On this page, the concerns from the first page were that they were like an eyesore. An eyesore means ugly. No one would want to look at those. But they said, "You might think they're ugly, but we're gonna go ahead with it." OK? See, there's like a contrast. There are two different things happening here. Some people don't want it. Some people want it. But they're going ahead with it.	• He elaborates on the contrast being described in the text by again referring to the word *concerns*.

Video Episode 2.3.2: "Turn and Talk"	Our Notes
Mr. W: OK. Let's keep going. This might throw a little twist into things. [reading] "But support for the turbines among the islanders is not quite as positive as before." I want to ask you a question as a reader 'cause we're all readers. When you see that word *but*, B-U-T, the first word of that paragraph, does that make you think what I'm thinking, that it's going to get more complicated here? Students: Yeah. Mr. W: Everything was going well. They even had extra energy that they could sell. And then what word pops up? Students: *But.* Mr. W: *But.* So things are going well, and then what, Deangelo? Deangelo: *But.* Mr. W: *But.* Something's not gonna go well. OK. On—[reading] "but support for the turbines among the islanders is not quite as positive as before. Unfortunately, wind turbines make noise. According to the people of Vinalhaven who live within a half-mile of the turbines, they make a lot of noise—so much that it causes anxiety and stress, and people nearby cannot sleep. Some neighbors say that the noise is no worse than the sound of passing traffic, or the waves on the ocean, or even the noise produced by the old power plant that has since been removed. They just had to get used to the noise, and now they hardly notice it. Animals, such as livestock on farms where wind turbines are installed, tend to do the same." That means they just get used to it after a while. "They are disturbed at first by the noise of the turbines, but they soon became accustomed to it and pay no attention." Mr. W: OK. Stay where you are. I mean, don't turn the—to the next page. I'm going to ask you to turn to a partner, to the person you looked at—you made eye contact with before. And we're hearing lots of examples about why people might be for wind turbines, why they would want them in their neighborhood or their communities, and why people might be against them. Try to talk about both reasons. I'm gonna give you maybe two minutes to talk, so try to talk about why people in this community might be for it and might be against it. OK? Start talking.	• Here, Mr. Weinberg refers to a specific word in the text (*but*) and explains how that word cues a reader that upcoming information in the text is going to complicate things. • He has students turn and talk as a way to sum up the arguments for and against wind turbines.

Video Episode 2.4: Working With Student Comments

We selected the last video episode for this chapter because it demonstrates how Mr. Weinberg elicits and uses student comments. Jot down what you notice as you watch the video episode noted below.

 2.4: Working With Student Comments (5:52)

Video Episode 2.4: Working With Student Comments	Our Notes
Mr. W: OK, give me five. Great, thank you. OK. I'm gonna try to write really quickly. I apologize. It's gonna be sloppy, but I want to just quickly write stuff down to, to capture some of the things we're talking about. What are some reasons people would be for wind turbines? Why would people want wind turbines? Someone we haven't heard from yet? Did you have a reason? Student: No. Mr. W: Not right now? Go ahead. Student: Like, like didn't it say before that people were saving money on electricity? They want it because of that. Mr. W: Saving money on electricity. Student: Mm-hmm. Mr. W: Great. Go ahead. Student: They might be for it because like she said, they could save money for electricity, but they can use the money for like things they might want, like to shop for clothes or to go out to dinners. Mr. W: That'd be great to have a little— Student: And just do what they want to. Mr. W: Have a little bit of extra money. And Deangelo was sharing with me that you still have all the power you had before, but now you've got some extra money. You can make some extra money. OK, let's get— I know that the list could probably go on and on. Let's just get one more thing up here, and then we'll do reasons why people might not want them. Precious? Precious: Because they might be for it 'cause— What was it that [inaudible] say? Because, because the— even though it— I forgot. Mr. W: Will you think of an against, and I'll call on you? OK. Cody, what were you going to say? Cody: Gonna say help the environment. Mr. W: Help the environment, right? And that's what we started talking about.	• During the "turn and talk" session, students shared the arguments for and against the use of wind turbines. As students talked together, Mr. Weinberg listened in on what they were saying. Later in this episode, he will use what one student said. • Writing students' contributions on the whiteboard demonstrates the value of their comments as well as the importance of sharing them with the group. • Organizing student comments into categories (for and against) provides a framework for thinking and talking about the ideas. • Here, Mr. Weinberg shares one of the comments he heard Deangelo make during "turn and talk." • Here, Mr. Weinberg supports Precious's effort to be part of the discussion by saying that he will call on her again and cueing her about what to be ready to talk about. *(continued)*

Video Episode 2.4: Working With Student Comments *continued*	Our Notes
Precious: Yeah, that's what it was. Mr. W: That's what you were gonna say, Precious? Precious: Yeah. Mr. W: Great. So we got it up there. Now, why don't people want them? Coolio, you got something? Coolio: Yes, because it made like too much noise for them to sleep. Mr. W: They're noisy. I remember what you said. I'm gonna wait to talk about it, though. Hugh, what do you think? Hugh: Like he said, like help the environment. It also says that it might destroy the environment. Mr. W: Do you remember what—why—what they thought it would destroy or why they thought it might destroy the environment? Hugh: I don't know. Mr. W: I'm not—I'm not even sure how clear it was in there. What was the worry about what it might do to animals or wildlife? Go ahead. Student: It creates pollution. Mr. W: Does it? Student: Yeah. Mr. W: Do you remember— Student: Because of the coal, and they used fuels. Mr. W: OK. Those were—so those were power plants that we talked about. Power plants are more like the electric—like the power stations, like the electric power plants. That's what they wanted to take away and put wind turbines in their place. So yes, those pollute. Power plants pollute. Some alliteration. Kitty? Kitty: It might disturb the livestock they said in there around the, around the wind turbines. Mr. W: Good. They might disturb livestock through the noise. This isn't—this wasn't in here yet, but I've heard about that. People—environmentalists are worried that it might affect birds and the patterns that birds fly in. Mr. W: One more thing and then I want to share something Deangelo said which I thought—which made me think of this in a different way. Octavius? Octavius: They said it caused anxiety and stress.	• Mr. Weinberg connects the student's comment about coal and using fuels to power plants. That focuses attention on the important idea that power plants and the pollution they create by burning fuels such as coal are being compared with wind turbines.

(continued)

Video Episode 2.4: Working With Student Comments *continued*	Our Notes
Mr. W: Yeah, it did say that. Like—and stress-inducing like I can't sleep. I'm sleepless. I'm so—this noise is different than any noise I knew before. Now I can't get any sleep, so now I'm going to work so stressed out. So and d—anxiety and stress-inducing, that means like causing.	• Mr. Weinberg elaborates on Octavius's comment.
Mr. W: Now, Deangelo said something that made me think of one of these, the against arguments. He reminded me that in the text, this one—it was a noisy one, right? It started off as an against, but then what? What did the people of this island do? What happened? You want to say it again? You tell us. Deangelo: They ignored it. Mr. W: They ignored it. So it was an against. It was a reason not to have them. But then all of a sudden, it sort of went away. I'm gonna put like a fuzzy line through that. It sort of went away. So it's a real reason people might be worried about it, might not want it, but then lo and behold, they got used to it. OK? Go ahead.	• Here, Mr. Weinberg begins to share Deangelo's comment with the class and asks him to complete the comment. • This move provides a very secure context for Deangelo to make a contribution.
Student: I was thinking about what you said about birds flying in different, different thing—not flying in the same way because I was thinking about that the turbine blade would like—when it flings around, that it chops the air. So maybe that's why.	• Interestingly, Mr. Weinberg's sharing of Deangelo's comment provides a way for this student to share a comment that Mr. Weinberg made previously.
Mr. W: That's really interesting. So birds get confused. The wind pattern is being changed, so they get confused. So the worry was that their migration pattern. So birds fly south in the winter from places like ours, like the Midwest, like Michigan, Illinois. And when the—they don't know how to get to where they wanted to go because wind turbines could affect the wind patterns.	• Mr. Weinberg interprets the student's comment and revoices it, or shapes the student's idea, so it is more understandable.
Mr. W: You're right. It's chopping it up in a different way. But it also—could it also be the noise that if their ears are picking up different sounds, they might get confused, too? Student: Yes. Mr. W: Could be. OK. Let's look at page 3. We're gonna start to hear how these things actually work. It's really compl—it's very complicated, but it's very cool.	

Chapter 2: Planning and Discussing "Harnessing the Wind"   43

Discussion Moves Demonstrated in the Video Episodes

We selected the video episodes that you viewed while reading this chapter to demonstrate the discussion moves summarized below:

- Video Episode 2.1: Launching the Discussion
  - Elicit and use students' prior knowledge.
  - Establish meaning of the keyword in the text's title.
  - Post questions to guide students' thinking about the text.
- Video Episode 2.2: Returning to the Text
  - Return to the text so student attention is focused on relevant information.
- Video Episodes 2.3.1: Language Cues
  - Direct student attention to language cues in the text: referents.
  - Elaborate on text information.
- Video Episode 2.3.2: "Turn and Talk"
  - Direct student attention to language cues in the text: contrastive connectives.
  - Use "turn and talk" so students can share ideas.
- Video Episode 2.4: Working With Student Comments
  - Select student comments during "turn and talk."
  - Capture and organize student comments in writing.
  - Provide support for student contributions.
  - Elaborate on student comments.
  - Revoice student comments.

Take It Away

As we mentioned earlier, we strongly recommend that you use the discussion plan for "Harnessing the Wind" with your students. Remember that you are free to make copies of the article for your students. Copy the discussion plan or write notes on your copy of the article. You may want to note key points on sticky notes and attach those to your copy of the article as well.

Audiotape or videotape your discussion. Capturing the discussion on audio or video is the only way that you will be able to review how the discussion unfolded. An even more effective way to analyze the discussion is by transcribing key sections. Teachers we have worked with have said that analyzing transcripts of their discussions has proved to be exceptionally powerful in informing their teaching.

Use the transcript analysis tools in Appendix A to guide your analysis.

CHAPTER 3

Planning and Discussing "Black Death"

*I*n this chapter, we focus on a discussion of the text "Black Death" by Janet Callahan. The chapter also includes video excerpts from a discussion of the text enacted by Ms. Erica Hatt and her fourth-grade class.

Careful Reading of the Text

Read "Black Death," which appears on the following pages. After reading, return to the text and take some notes. Consider opportunities and challenges that the text presents related to important content, useful text features, and understanding aspects of disciplinary knowledge. Again, we suggest that you underline and make notes on a copy of the text and use sticky notes to mark important parts.

Black Death

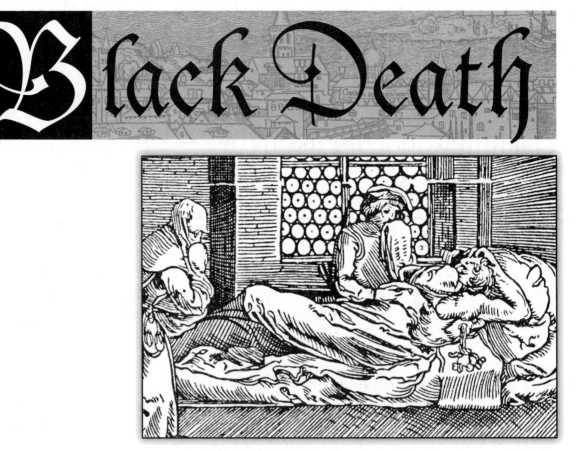

by Janet Callahan

In 1347, a deadly disease swept across Europe. People did not know what caused it. They did not know how to treat it, either. As a result, 25 million people died within five years. About 40 percent of Europe's population was wiped out.

This terrible disease became known as the Black Death. This name suggests the fear that gripped Europe as the disease spread. It also describes the disease's most unmistakable sign: the black or dark purple spots that appeared on victims' bodies before they died.

THE 'BLACK DEATH'
ENTERED ENGLAND IN 1348
THROUGH THIS PORT.

IT KILLED 30–50%
OF THE COUNTRY'S
TOTAL POPULATION.

Plaque displayed in Weymouth, England

Flea
(actual size = 1/16 inch, or about 1.5 mm)

Most experts believed the Black Death was caused by a germ called *Yersinia pestis*. In 2011, scientists studying centuries-old skeletons confirmed that the experts were right about this germ. The germ lived in the bodies of fleas that attached themselves to rats. In the 1300s, rats were a part of everyday life in the cities and villages of Europe. They lived in streets and alleys. They lived in people's homes. Infected fleas that bit people passed the disease on to them. People could also catch the disease by coming in close contact with someone who had already fallen ill.

Historians have studied how Black Death germs arrived in Europe. Many believe the flea-ridden rats came from China to Europe on trade ships. Why do they think so? They know that just a few years before the Black Death struck Europe,

the same deadly disease broke out in China. Historians think that the flea-ridden rats got aboard European trade ships that visited Chinese ports. When the ships returned to Europe, they brought the rats—and the disease—with them.

Arrival of European trade ships

There is a convincing piece of evidence for this theory. It is an account of an eyewitness from Sicily, an island in the Mediterranean Sea off the coast of Italy. According to this account, a fleet of trade ships arrived in Sicily in October 1347. Many of the ships' crewmen were already dead when the ships docked. Many more were sick with the disease. When the people of Sicily realized that the Black Death had reached their shores, they ordered the ships out of the harbor. This action came too late to save the people of Sicily, however.

The Spread of Black Death in Europe, 1347–1350

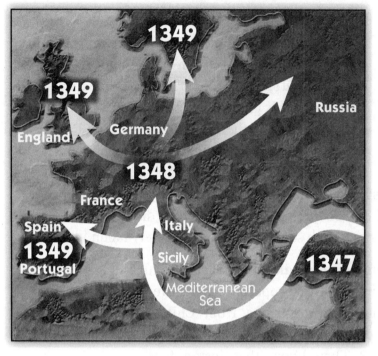

Within days, Sicilians began to come down with the disease. Before long, the Black Death reached other cities along the Mediterranean coast. Historical documents record that the disease spread inland with terrifying speed. It spread through France, Germany, Spain, and Portugal. It moved on to the British Isles and Scandinavia. It even reached the island of Greenland, near the North Pole, almost wiping out its population.

People felt helpless in the face of such a deadly disease. Although they did not know how to prevent the Black Death, they were willing to try almost anything. Some people washed walls and furniture and even their bodies with rose water or vinegar. Others tried to ward off the illness by wearing garlands of flowers. Many people believed they could stay healthy if they did not eat, drink, or exercise too much.

None of these precautions worked. Although a tiny fraction of people who fell ill with the disease were able to recover, most died within a week after their first symptoms appeared. The Black Death began with fever and chills. Before long, swellings appeared on the victim's neck and armpits. These swellings were called "buboes," and the disease is often referred to as bubonic plague. The swellings quickly spread over the entire body. Finally, the black or purple spots appeared, signaling that death was very near.

People who practiced medicine in the 1300s did not know much about diseases or how to treat them. The Black Death was often treated with a warm preparation of butter, onion, and garlic applied to the skin, but it did not help. The most popular remedy of the time was bloodletting, or leeching. In this treatment, the doctor tried to get rid of a disease by taking blood from the patient's body. But this procedure had no effect on the Black Death.

The fear and panic that came with the Black Death was almost as destructive as the death toll. When the Black Death struck a town or village, those who were still healthy often fled for their lives. In the blink of an eye, a town would be left without its shop owners, craftsmen, and other workers. In this way, the Black Death wiped out whole communities.

By 1351, the Black Death had mostly vanished from Europe. In the next 150 years, there would be several more outbreaks of the disease, but none was as bad as the first. Yet fearful memories of the disease's first wave lingered for many years before Europeans finally believed that they had put the Black Death behind them for good.

Medical treatment included the use of leeches to remove "bad" blood from patients.

Reading the Text: Our Notes

Compare your notes to our notes below.

Text	Our Notes
page 1	
Black Death by Janet Callahan In 1347, a deadly disease swept across Europe. People did not know what caused it. They did not know how to treat it, either. As a result, 25 million people died within five years. About 40 percent of Europe's population was wiped out.	• The woodcut on this page depicts a gruesome scene: A person appears to be in agony, and there seems to be something coming out of the side of his body. • It is important that students understand that 1347 is almost 700 years ago. • The paragraph presents a stunning detail: Almost half of Europe's population was wiped out by a disease over a five-year period. The photograph of the plaque reinforces this statistic. The range of 30–50% indicates that this is an estimate, which makes sense. It would have been difficult to create and preserve careful records at that time.
This terrible disease became known as the Black Death. This name suggests the fear that gripped Europe as the disease spread. It also describes the disease's most unmistakable sign: the black or dark purple spots that appeared on victims' bodies before they died.	
page 2	
Most experts believed the Black Death was caused by a germ called *Yersinia pestis*. In 2011, scientists studying centuries-old skeletons confirmed that the experts were right about this germ. The germ lived in the bodies of fleas that attached themselves to rats. In the 1300s, rats were a part of everyday life in the cities and villages of Europe. They lived in streets and alleys. They lived in people's homes. Infected fleas that bit people passed the disease on to them. People could also catch the disease by coming in close contact with someone who had already fallen ill.	• The word choice here is important to note: experts *believed*, scientists *confirmed*. • This paragraph describes a causal chain linking the germ *Yersinia pestis* to people getting sick with the Black Death: (a) germs were in the bodies of fleas, (b) the fleas became attached to rats, (c) the rats carried the fleas into populated areas, (d) the fleas became attached to people, (e) the fleas bit the people and infected them with the germ, (f) people then infected one another. • We did some research about this and discovered that blood is the food of fleas. The rats provided that food. Fleas could have been carried by other animals, but rats were available, so they became the carriers. People, too, could carry fleas to other people they encountered. • Ms. Hatt created a paper chain to use as a reference point for students as they described the links in the causal chain. *(continued)*

Text	Our Notes
Historians have studied how Black Death germs arrived in Europe. Many believe the flea-ridden rats came from China to Europe on trade ships. Why do they think so? They know that just a few years before the Black Death struck Europe, the same deadly disease broke out in China. Historians think that the flea-ridden rats got aboard European trade ships that visited Chinese ports. When the ships returned to Europe, they brought the rats—and the disease—with them.	• This paragraph introduces historians and how they created an account that placed events on a causal chain explaining how the germ got from China to Europe. • The author's use of the words *believe* and *think* are noteworthy here. These words indicate that there is no certainty regarding how the disease spread. • The author uses a question to focus attention on the information that historians *do* have: knowledge about the outbreak of the disease in China and the trade routes that European ships used in the 14th century to transport goods from China to Europe. Tracing the trade route on a map would be useful here. • The last sentence focuses on the rats and the disease, but the link between the rats carrying the fleas with the germ is not mentioned. • *Flea-ridden* is an interesting term. Students may think it means that the fleas were riding on the rats. *Flea-ridden* means infested or covered with fleas.
There is a convincing piece of evidence for this theory. It is an account of an eyewitness from Sicily, an island in the Mediterranean Sea off the coast of Italy. According to this account, a fleet of trade ships arrived in Sicily in October 1347. Many of the ships' crewmen were already dead when the ships docked. Many more were sick with the disease. When the people of Sicily realized that the Black Death had reached their shores, they ordered the ships out of the harbor. This action came too late to save the people of Sicily, however.	• Here the words *evidence*, *theory*, and *eyewitness* are used. These need to be explained. • It's interesting that the author wrote, "When the people of Sicily realized…." It seems that people already knew about the disease. • Ms. Hatt explained a theory as "a working idea or an explanation that takes into account the available information." • Showing a map of Sicily and tracing the route from China to the island is important. (*continued*)

Text	Our Notes
page 3	
Within days, Sicilians began to come down with the disease. Before long, the Black Death reached other cities along the Mediterranean coast. Historical documents record that the disease spread inland with terrifying speed. It spread through France, Germany, Spain, and Portugal. It moved on to the British Isles and Scandinavia. It even reached the island of Greenland, near the North Pole, almost wiping out its population.	• The author refers to historical documents, which might have been census records or tax rolls. These documents would show the decline in population. • The woodcuts in the text are also historical documents. • The map on this page is useful for showing how the Black Death spread and also how long that took.
People felt helpless in the face of such a deadly disease. Although they did not know how to prevent the Black Death, they were willing to try almost anything. Some people washed walls and furniture and even their bodies with rose water or vinegar. Others tried to ward off the illness by wearing garlands of flowers. Many people believed they could stay healthy if they did not eat, drink, or exercise too much.	• This paragraph switches to a new topic: how people tried to prevent the spread of the disease. What the people did reveals something about the theories that people had about how the disease behaved and what might be causing it. For example, washing walls and furniture indicates that they might have thought that something like vinegar would destroy the disease. The use of rose water and garlands might indicate that they believed that scent might somehow keep the disease away.
None of these precautions worked. Although a tiny fraction of people who fell ill with the disease were able to recover, most died within a week after their first symptoms appeared. The Black Death began with fever and chills. Before long, swellings appeared on the victim's neck and armpits. These swellings were called "buboes," and the disease is often referred to as bubonic plague. The swellings quickly spread over the entire body. Finally, the black or purple spots appeared, signaling that death was very near.	• This paragraph reveals that the precautions people tried did not work. • Most people who caught the disease died, and they died quickly. • Details about the progress of the disease are graphically described.
page 4	
People who practiced medicine in the 1300s did not know much about diseases or how to treat them. The Black Death was often treated with a warm preparation of butter, onion, and garlic applied to the skin, but it did not help. The most popular remedy of the time was bloodletting, or leeching. In this treatment, the doctor tried to get rid of a disease by taking blood from the patient's body. But this procedure had no effect on the Black Death.	• This paragraph shifts attention from the efforts of ordinary people to the efforts of those who practiced medicine. The remedies used indicate the theories that the medical people held. • The woodcut illustration on this page clearly shows the leeches and how they were used. *(continued)*

Text	Our Notes
page 4 *continued*	
The fear and panic that came with the Black Death was almost as destructive as the death toll. When the Black Death struck a town or village, those who were still healthy often fled for their lives. In the blink of an eye, a town would be left without its shop owners, craftsmen, and other workers. In this way, the Black Death wiped out whole communities.	• The first sentence indicates the shift to a new topic: the effect of the Black Death on towns and villages when people left.
By 1351, the Black Death had mostly vanished from Europe. In the next 150 years, there would be several more outbreaks of the disease, but none was as bad as the first. Yet fearful memories of the disease's first wave lingered for many years before Europeans finally believed that they had put the Black Death behind them for good.	

Analyzing "Black Death"

We analyzed "Black Death" by focusing on important content, useful text features, and opportunities to develop disciplinary knowledge.

Content

"Black Death" presents important information about what the Black Death was and how it spread from China to Europe in the mid-1300s. It also describes the precautions and remedies used by people who lived during that time and the dire consequences of the disease in terms of death and the destruction of towns and villages.

Although there are no headings in the text, there are distinct sections or chunks of information:

- Section 1 (page 1)
  - When the Black Death infected Europe, the death toll, and what the disease was like
- Section 2 (page 2)
  - The discovery of scientists that the germ *Yersinia pestis* causes the the Black Death
  - The account that historians developed describing the causal chain linking the germ and its arrival in Europe

Research

We had some questions about the causal chain and did some research to make sure that we got it right. We discovered that fleas live on the blood of their hosts. On the ships that traveled from China to Europe, the fleas lived on the blood of the rats. In the contained space of a ship, the fleas also fed on the sailors. When the ships arrived in Sicily, many sailors were dead and many others sick. The disease spread because there were many flea-ridden rats and flea-ridden sailors who survived the voyage. The rats, however, were the main carriers of the fleas, which carried the disease into the European population. There is no agreed-upon explanation about how the germ developed in China.

Text Features

The text provides opportunities for focusing on important language cues and graphics.

- *Language cues:* The author's word choice provides important cues for readers in making inferences about the thinking of scientists and historians. These words include *believed/confirmed* and *believe/think.* Between believing and confirming, scientists discovered evidence (the germ *Yersinia pestis* was discovered in the bones of skeletons from the time of the Black Death). Between believing and thinking, historians made use of evidence in the form of eyewitness accounts and historical documents.

- *Graphics:* The photograph on page 1, the woodcuts on pages 1 and 2, and the map on page 3 enhance information provided in the text.

Disciplinary Knowledge

The text provides an opportunity for students to learn about the work of scientists and historians in developing causal chains that describe how historical events are related. The text describes how scientists secured evidence about the cause of the Black Death: analyzing skeletons and discovering the germ *Yersinia pestis.* The text also explains how historians used an eyewitness report, historical records, and knowledge of trade routes to develop an account explaining how the disease spread.

Selecting Learning Goals

Selecting learning goals for reading and discussing a text is the next step in developing a discussion plan. Here are the learning goals that we selected for "Black Death":

1. What was the Black Death, and what did it cause?

    The Black Death was a disease that spread throughout Europe in the 14th century, killing 40% of the population.

2. What did people's actions reveal about what they believed about preventing and treating the disease?

    People of the time used precautions and remedies that they believed would stop or cure the disease. These efforts reveal the working theories that people had back then about how the disease spread and what might cure it.

3. How did scientists and historians make use of evidence to develop a causal chain to explain the cause and spread of the Black Death?

    Scientists analyzed skeletons of people who died from the Black Death and discovered the germ *Yersinia pestis,* the first link in the causal chain. Historians studied eyewitness accounts and historical documents and used their knowledge of trade routes to explain subsequent events in the causal chain:

    The germ *Yersinia pestis* was in fleas.

    ↓

    The fleas infected rats.

    ↓

The flea-infested rats traveled on ships from China to Sicily and other European ports.

↓

The rats left the ships and became part of European towns.

↓

The fleas on the rats jumped onto people and bit them.

↓

The germ infected people.

↓

Infected people spread the disease to other people.

↓

People became sick and died.

4. What word choices do authors make to convey the status of information?

The word *confirm* indicates that a fact has been established. The words *think* and *believe* indicate theories, or ideas, that have yet to be proven.

5. How can illustrations, photographs, and maps help readers understand text information?

The photograph on page 1, the woodcuts on pages 1 and 2, and the map on page 3 enhance information provided in the text.

The first learning goal targets the essential content in the text: what the Black Death was and what it caused. The second focuses students' attention on the theories that people of the time had about what caused the disease and how it could be prevented and treated. This is a more sophisticated goal than simply describing what people did. The third focuses attention on the work of historians and how they use various sources to develop a causal chain to explain events. The fourth directs students to notice important language cues. The fifth foregrounds the importance of graphics in comprehending an informational text.

Designing the Exit

Given the learning goals, we designed the following exit activity. We think the activity engages students in synthesizing the important text content.

Provide chart paper and markers and have students work in small groups to:

• Describe what they think is going on in the woodcut on page 1

• Create a causal chain linking the events leading up to the scene in the woodcut

Designing the Launch

We planned a simple launch for the discussion:

• Distribute copies of "Black Death." Read the title, author, and first two paragraphs.

• Indicate the location of Europe and England on a world map.

As we read and talk about this article, we'll learn more about this deadly disease, but what have we learned so far?

Designing the Discussion Plan

In the section that follows, we show how our analysis of "Black Death" and the learning that we selected informed the design of a discussion plan for reading and talking about the text.

As in Chapter 2, the words in *italics* are what we would say to students. We provide the discussion plan not as a script but as an example of how we would support students in comprehending the important text ideas and organizing those ideas into a coherent mental representation.

Discussion Plan for "Black Death"

Learning Goals

1. What was the Black Death, and what did it cause?

   The Black Death was a disease that spread throughout Europe in the 14th century, killing 40% of the population.

2. What did people's actions reveal about what they believed about preventing and treating the disease?

   People of the time used precautions and remedies that they believed would stop or cure the disease. These efforts reveal the working theories that people had back then about how the disease spread and what might cure it.

3. How did scientists and historians make use of evidence to develop a causal chain to explain the cause and spread of the Black Death?

   Scientists analyzed skeletons of people who died from the Black Death and discovered the germ *Yersinia pestis*, the first link in the causal chain. Historians studied eyewitness accounts and historical documents and used their knowledge of trade routes to explain subsequent events in the causal chain:

   The germ *Yersinia pestis* was in fleas.

   ↓

   The fleas infected rats.

   ↓

   The flea-infested rats traveled on ships from China to Sicily and other European ports.

   ↓

   The rats left the ships and became part of European towns.

   ↓

   The fleas on the rats jumped onto people and bit them.

   ↓

   The germ infected people.

   ↓

   Infected people spread the disease to other people.

   ↓

   People became sick and died.

4. What word choices do authors make to convey the status of information?

The word *confirm* indicates that a fact has been established. The words *think* and *believe* indicate theories, or ideas, that have yet to be proven.

5. How can illustrations, photographs, and maps help readers understand text information?

The photograph on page 1, the woodcuts on pages 1 and 2, and the map on page 3 enhance information provided in the text.

Resources

- Copies of "Black Death"
- World map
- A paper chain with eight links
- Chart paper and markers

Launch

Distribute copies of "Black Death." Read the title, author, and first two paragraphs. Indicate the location of Europe and England on a world map.

As we read and talk about this informational article, we will learn more about this deadly disease, but what have we learned so far?

The **bolded** text in the table below provides instructions for what you should do. Instructions to read, for example, mean that you or a volunteer should read the indicated text aloud.

Text	Our Notes	Reader–Text Interactions
page 1		
Black Death by Janet Callahan In 1347, a deadly disease swept across Europe. People did not know what caused it. They did not know how to treat it, either. As a result, 25 million people died within five years. About 40 percent of Europe's population was wiped out.	• The woodcut on this page depicts a gruesome scene: A person appears to be in agony, and there seems to be something coming out of the side of his body. • It is important that students understand that 1347 is almost 700 years ago. • The paragraph presents a stunning detail: Almost half of Europe's population was wiped out by a disease over a five-year period. The photograph of the plaque reinforces this statistic. The range of 30–50% indicates that this is an estimate, which makes sense. It would have been difficult to create and preserve careful records at that time.	• **Refer to a world map and indicate Europe.** • *Let's think about the statistic here: "about 40 percent of Europe's population was wiped out." That's 4 out of every 10 people. Count off by 10s. Four in every group would be dead if we were living in 1347 in Europe.* • **Indicate the location of England on the world map. Explain that the plaque refers to the effect of the Black Death in England.** • *Look at the plaque in the photograph on this page. Why do you think it says 30–50%? That's quite a range.* *(continued)*

Text	Our Notes	Reader–Text Interactions
page 1 *continued*		
This terrible disease became known as the Black Death. This name suggests the fear that gripped Europe as the disease spread. It also describes the disease's most unmistakable sign: the black or dark purple spots that appeared on victims' bodies before they died.		
page 2		
Most experts believed the Black Death was caused by a germ called *Yersinia pestis*. In 2011, scientists studying centuries-old skeletons confirmed that the experts were right about this germ. The germ lived in the bodies of fleas that attached themselves to rats. In the 1300s, rats were a part of everyday life in the cities and villages of Europe. They lived in streets and alleys. They lived in people's homes. Infected fleas that bit people passed the disease on to them. People could also catch the disease by coming in close contact with someone who had already fallen ill.	• The word choice here is important to note: experts *believed*, scientists *confirmed*. • This paragraph describes a causal chain linking the germ *Yersinia pestis* to people getting sick with the Black Death: (a) germs were in the bodies of fleas, (b) the fleas became attached to rats, (c) the rats carried the fleas into populated areas, (d) the fleas became attached to people, (e) the fleas bit the people and infected them with the germ, (f) people then infected one another. • We did some research about this and discovered that blood is the food of fleas. The rats provided that food. Fleas could have been carried by other animals, but rats were available, so they became the carriers. People, too, could carry fleas to other people they encountered. • Ms. Hatt created a paper chain to use as a reference point for students as they described the links in the causal chain.	• **Read the first two sentences.** • *The author wrote, "experts believed" and "scientists...confirmed." What does it mean to confirm something? For example, a doctor might administer some tests to confirm that a person has a particular virus or bacterium in his or her blood. What's the difference between the words* believed *and* confirmed? *(Evidence is the key difference.)* • **Read the rest of the paragraph.** • *So what did we learn about the germ and how people got the Black Death? What are the key events that can be linked together in a causal chain to explain the connection between the germ and how people got the Black Death?* • **Show the paper chain and encourage students to explain key links:** • Fleas on rats bit people. • Germs infected people. • Infected people spread the disease to other people. • People became sick and died. *(continued)*

Text	Our Notes	Reader–Text Interactions

Historians have studied how Black Death germs arrived in Europe. Many believe the flea-ridden rats came from China to Europe on trade ships. Why do they think so? They know that just a few years before the Black Death struck Europe, the same deadly disease broke out in China. Historians think that the flea-ridden rats got aboard European trade ships that visited Chinese ports. When the ships returned to Europe, they brought the rats—and the disease—with them.	• This paragraph introduces historians and how they created an account that placed events on a causal chain explaining how the germ got from China to Europe.
	• The author's use of the words *believe* and *think* are noteworthy here. These words indicate that there is no certainty regarding how the disease spread.
	• The author uses a question to focus attention on the information that historians *do* have: knowledge about the outbreak of the disease in China and the trade routes that European ships used in the 14th century to transport goods from China to Europe. Tracing the trade route on a map would be useful here.
	• The last sentence focuses on the rats and the disease, but the link between the rats carrying the fleas with the germ is not mentioned.
	• *Flea-ridden* is an interesting term. Students may think it means that the fleas were riding on the rats. *Flea-ridden* means infested or covered with fleas.
		• **Read the paragraph.**
		• *Here we learn about how historians put together information to create an account of how the Black Death spread.*
		• *What words in this paragraph are cues that the historians are not certain about how they have explained the events?*
		• *Using this chain again, what are the links that historians are proposing to connect the spread of the Black Death from China to Europe?*
		• **Show the paper chain and ask students to explain key links:**
		  • The germ was in fleas in China.
		  • Fleas infected rats.
		  • Rats traveled to Europe on ships.
		  • Rats left ships and went into towns.
		• *What information did historians use to develop this chain of events?*
		
		(continued)

Text	Our Notes	Reader–Text Interactions
page 2 continued		
There is a convincing piece of evidence for this theory. It is an account of an eyewitness from Sicily, an island in the Mediterranean Sea off the coast of Italy. According to this account, a fleet of trade ships arrived in Sicily in October 1347. Many of the ships' crewmen were already dead when the ships docked. Many more were sick with the disease. When the people of Sicily realized that the Black Death had reached their shores, they ordered the ships out of the harbor. This action came too late to save the people of Sicily, however.	• Here the words *evidence*, *theory*, and *eyewitness* are used. These need to be explained. • It's interesting that the author wrote, "When the people of Sicily realized…." It seems that people already knew about the disease. • Ms. Hatt explained a theory as "a working idea or an explanation that takes into account the available information." • Showing a map of Sicily and tracing the route from China to the island is important.	• **Read the paragraph.** • *Here we read about a convincing piece of evidence that supports the historians' theory about how the Black Death spread from China to Europe.* • *A theory "is a working idea or an explanation that takes into account the available information." What was the available information, or evidence, that supports the historians' theory about how the Black Death spread to Europe?* • **Show the water route from China to Sicily on the world map.**
page 3		
Within days, Sicilians began to come down with the disease. Before long, the Black Death reached other cities along the Mediterranean coast. Historical documents record that the disease spread inland with terrifying speed. It spread through France, Germany, Spain, and Portugal. It moved on to the British Isles and Scandinavia. It even reached the island of Greenland, near the North Pole, almost wiping out its population.	• The author refers to historical documents, which might have been census records or tax rolls. These documents would show the decline in population. • The woodcuts in the text are also historical documents. • The map on this page is useful for showing how the Black Death spread and also how long that took.	• **Read the paragraph.** • *The author mentions historical documents here. These documents might have been census records or tax rolls. These documents would show the decline in population.* • *The woodcuts in the text are also historical documents.* • *What important information can we learn from the map on this page?* *(continued)*

Text	Our Notes	Reader–Text Interactions

page 3 continued

| People felt helpless in the face of such a deadly disease. Although they did not know how to prevent the Black Death, they were willing to try almost anything. Some people washed walls and furniture and even their bodies with rose water or vinegar. Others tried to ward off the illness by wearing garlands of flowers. Many people believed they could stay healthy if they did not eat, drink, or exercise too much. | • This paragraph switches to a new topic: how people tried to prevent the spread of the disease. What the people did reveals something about the theories that people had about how the disease behaved and what might be causing it. For example, washing walls and furniture indicates that they might have thought that something like vinegar would destroy the disease. The use of rose water and garlands might indicate that they believed that scent might somehow keep the disease away. | • **Read the paragraph.**
• *We've been reading about how the Black Death got to Europe and infected people. Now the author is focusing our attention on what people did to try to prevent the spread of the disease.*
• *Let's connect what people did with what they might have been thinking. People did things like washing walls and furniture because they had theories, or ideas, about what might prevent the disease. What might those theories have been?* |
| None of these precautions worked. Although a tiny fraction of people who fell ill with the disease were able to recover, most died within a week after their first symptoms appeared. The Black Death began with fever and chills. Before long, swellings appeared on the victim's neck and armpits. These swellings were called "buboes," and the disease is often referred to as bubonic plague. The swellings quickly spread over the entire body. Finally, the black or purple spots appeared, signaling that death was very near. | • This paragraph reveals that the precautions people tried did not work.
• Most people who caught the disease died, and they died quickly.
• Details about the progress of the disease are graphically described. | • **Read the paragraph.**
• *What happened to people who became infected with the disease?* |

page 4

| People who practiced medicine in the 1300s did not know much about diseases or how to treat them. The Black Death was often treated with a warm preparation of butter, onion, and garlic applied to the skin, but it did not help. The most popular remedy of the time was bloodletting, or leeching. In this treatment, the doctor tried to get rid of a disease by taking blood from the patient's body. But this procedure had no effect on the Black Death. | • This paragraph shifts attention from the efforts of ordinary people to the efforts of those who practiced medicine. The remedies used indicate the theories that the medical people held.
• The woodcut illustration on this page clearly shows the leeches and how they were used. | • **Read the paragraph.**
• *What does this paragraph focus on?*
• *What do the treatments reveal about the theories of the people who practiced medicine back then?*

(continued) |

Text	Our Notes	Reader–Text Interactions
page 4 *continued*		
The fear and panic that came with the Black Death was almost as destructive as the death toll. When the Black Death struck a town or village, those who were still healthy often fled for their lives. In the blink of an eye, a town would be left without its shop owners, craftsmen, and other workers. In this way, the Black Death wiped out whole communities.	• The first sentence indicates the shift to a new topic: the effect of the Black Death on towns and villages when people left.	• **Read the paragraph.** • *We have read that the Black Death caused the deaths of many people. What was the effect of the Black Death on healthy people?*
By 1351, the Black Death had mostly vanished from Europe. In the next 150 years, there would be several more outbreaks of the disease, but none was as bad as the first. Yet fearful memories of the disease's first wave lingered for many years before Europeans finally believed that they had put the Black Death behind them for good.		• **Read the paragraph.** • *It's easy to imagine that people would long remember the effects of such a devastating event as the Black Death.*

Exit

Provide chart paper and markers and have students work in small groups to:

- Describe what they think is going on in the woodcut on page 1
- Create a causal chain linking the events leading up to the scene in the woodcut

Some Important Moves in the Discussion Plan

Here we describe some of the discussion moves that we used in the discussion plan for "Black Death."

- *Foregrounding the disciplinary work of scientists and historians:* The text provides excellent examples of scientists and historians using evidence to develop and, when possible, confirm their theories. We extended the concept of theorizing by asking students to speculate about the theories informing the precautions and remedies developed by people living during the Black Death.

- *Focusing on language cues:* The text also provides excellent examples of how word choice conveys important information. Specifically, the words, *think, believe,* and *confirm* indicate degrees of confidence and certainty.

Viewing Video Episodes

The video episodes for this chapter feature Ms. Hatt and her class of fourth graders discussing the text "Black Death."

Video Episode 3.1: Scaffolding Student Thinking

As you watch this video episode, notice how Ms. Hatt scaffolds students' thinking. Jot down your observations and then compare them with our notes in the table below.

 3.1: Scaffolding Student Thinking (4:33)

Video Episode 3.1: Scaffolding Student Thinking	Our Notes
Ms. H: We're at the top paragraph that begins with *most*. [reading] "Most experts believed the Black Death was caused by a germ called *Yersinia pestis*. The germ lived in the bodies of fleas that attached themselves to rats. In the 1300s, rats were a part of everyday life in the cities and villages of Europe. They lived in streets and alleys. They lived in people's homes. Infected fleas that bit people passed the disease on to them. People could also catch the disease by coming in close contact with someone who had already fallen ill." Let's stop right there. Historians explain events in history by putting them on a causal chain, by talking about how they are linked to one another. I have a chain here to show you what I mean. This chain is made up of links. This link is connected to this link, which is then connected to this one and then this one. Ms. H: That's what historians do with events in history. They talk about one event and how it directly connects to another event, or leads to another event, and how that event leads to another. Shawn? Shawn: Sort of like detectives or policemen. Ms. H: Oh, how they find one clue and then move on to the next? Shawn: Yeah [inaudible]. Ms. H: Exactly. Actually, I think the historians are definitely detectives. Yes, Kaleel? Kaleel: Or I agree with Shawn or like a bomb squad trying to find a bomb.	• Ms. Hatt scaffolds student thinking by using a paper chain to demonstrate the linking of events on a causal chain. The chain makes concrete the abstract concept of a causal chain. • Ms. Hatt also scaffolds student thinking by her consistent use of the terms *causal chain*, *chain*, *links*, *link*, *events*, and *connected*. *(continued)*

Video Episode 3.1: Scaffolding Student Thinking *continued*	Our Notes
Ms. H: OK, yeah. So doing a lot of investigating, right? So I want to talk about the causal chain in this text so far. I want to talk about the chain that links the germ and people falling ill. What links are in between those two events? We're starting with the germ, *Yersinia pestis*, and ending with people falling ill. What are the links in this chain? What are the events that are connected to one another?	
Ms. H: If you're not quite sure, you may want to look back at that paragraph that starts with "Most experts believe." Go ahead, Lynn.	• Cueing students to return to the text is another form of scaffolding.
Lynn: First, the germ gets into a flea's body, and the fleas latch onto rats. Then, the rats like go into the pers—somebody's house, and the flea jumps off the rat and bites someone.	• This student describes the causal chain correctly.
Ms. H: OK. Does anybody want to add to that? Mary?	
Mary: That, that— Like Lynn said, a flea would like, a flea would just have the disease on him sort of like a fly has diseases on it. Then, it jumps somewhere, spreads the disease there, and then if that person has it, it's gonna spread to the next person and the next person and the next person, like a cold.	• Mary focuses on the last sentence in the paragraph, which extends, or adds on to, the first student's description.
Ms. H: The author gave us some information about rats. How were rats involved? Shawn?	• Ms. Hatt does not address the addition but refocuses on the key role of the rats.
Shawn: They're involved because most fleas are really small, so most fleas jump on bigger animals to sort of catch rides and eat stuff. So they would jump on a rat, and then a rat would live in like an alley or your house or even a city or a village. And so then maybe if somebody found one, they might get the disease. Or if a flea jumped off and touched something, and the— then a person grabbed that thing, they might get the disease also.	• Shawn incorporates the information about the role of both rats and people in spreading the disease.
Ms. H: Mm-hmm. And it says here that during this time, rats were very much a part of everyday life. It says here that they lived in the streets and alleys and even in people's homes. That's much different than it is today. OK. Let's move on.	• Ms. Hatt reinforces the description by returning to the text to emphasize the rats and their presence in people's surroundings.

Video Episode 3.2: *More Examples of Scaffolding*

As you watch this next video episode, notice how Ms. Hatt continues to scaffold students' thinking. Again, jot down your observations and then compare your notes with ours.

 3.2: More Examples of Scaffolding (7:18)

Video Episode 3.2: More Examples of Scaffolding	Our Notes
Ms. H: Second paragraph. [reading] "Experts have studied how Black Death germs arrived in Europe. Many believe the flea-ridden rats came from China to Europe on trade ships. Why do they think so? They know that just a few years before the Black Death struck Europe, the same deadly disease broke out in China. Experts think that the flea-ridden," or infested, that's what *flea-ridden* means, "rats got aboard European trade ships that visited Chinese ports. When the ships returned to Europe, they brought the rats—and the disease—with them." The author just gave us more links on this causal chain we were talking about. Let me show you on this map. The text said that experts believe that flea-ridden rats got onboard ships that were in China, and then the ships traveled until they got to Europe. And actually we'll find out that it was first Sicily that they arrived to. We're gonna move on to that third paragraph on the page that starts with "There is." Ms. H: [reading] "There is a convincing piece of evidence for this theory. It is an account of an eyewitness from Sicily, an island in the Mediterranean Sea off the coast of Italy. According to this account," which is a description of events— I lost my place. Oh, "a fleet of trade ships arrived in Sicily in October 1347. Many of the ships' crewmen were already dead when the ship docked. Many more were sick with the disease. When the people of Sicily realized that the Black Death had reached their shores, they ordered the ships out of the harbor. This action came too late to save the people of Sicily, however." [turns page to next paragraph] "Within days, Sicilians began to come down with the disease before long—" Oh, I'm sorry, "with the disease. Before long, the Black Death reached other cities along the Mediterranean coast." From there, it "spread inland with terrifying speed. It spread through France, Germany, Spain, and Portugal. It moved on to the British Isles and Scandinavia. It even reached the island of Greenland, near the North Pole, almost wiping out the population."	• Ms. Hatt connects the information in this paragraph to information from the previous paragraph, reinforcing the connection by referring once again to the keywords *links* and *causal chain*.

(continued)

Video Episode 3.2: More Examples of Scaffolding *continued*	Our Notes
Ms. H: You may think, boys and girls, that only scientists talk about theories, but historians also talk about theories. A theory—I have it up here for you to see because I've been saying that word so often—is a working idea or an explanation that takes into account the available information. So scientists and historians make theories. And the—so what the theory—so what is a theory that the historians have developed so far about the arrival of this germ to Europe? What is the explanation, or working idea, of how this Black Death germ arrived in Europe? What has the author told us so far? Aveeni?	• Here, Ms. Hatt focuses students' attention on the word *theory*. She refers to the explanation of *theory* that she has written on chart paper: "a working idea or an explanation that takes into account available information."
Aveeni: That it's been traveling from different places, and it's been coming from other places that came to Europe.	• She then links scientists and historians and their use of theories. And she uses the word *theory* again and its explanation to ask students about what theory the historians had developed about the germ and its arrival in Europe.
Ms. H: Aveeni, say more.	
Aveeni: That probably it does, it— It's kind of like something go from one place to another, and it hops to different places. Like from Urrup—Europe, it went to other places, and then it circled around all the places near Europe.	
Ms. H: Can somebody add to that and tell us more about this theory, this explanation of how they arrived to Europe? Mary?	• Here again, Ms. Hatt uses the words *theory* and *explanation*. That's what she wants students to talk about.
Mary: First, it was in China, and then like trading ships are going back and forth, and like mice got onto the sailing ships with—and they had the fleas on them. And when they went to England, the fleas got them. Now they're spreading it all over.	
Ms. H: OK. Shawn, do you have something to add?	
Shawn: Maybe the—maybe the, the rats that got on the ship were—smelled like food or they were hungry, so they would go to the food. And then the food might have gotten poisoned or might have gotten the disease, and then it would have spread across the boat and then to the mainland.	*(continued)*

Video Episode 3.2: More Examples of Scaffolding *continued*	Our Notes
Ms. H: So it sounds like you are forming your own theory about what happened on the boat, right? However, the author told us very specific information about the theory that historians have, and they also provided us with some evidence. We're gonna have to go back, probably to the last page, to find that evidence. But I would like us to talk about what evidence supported the theory that historians had that this germ came from China. What's the evidence? I'm turning back to page 2. That last paragraph might have some information for us. We need evidence. Maria?	• Here, Ms. Hatt labels Shawn's thinking as a theory. • Here, Ms. Hatt connects theory and evidence and directs students to return to the text to find the evidence that historians used. She models returning to the text by doing just that.
Maria: [Inaudible] was caused, was caused in China.	
Ms. H: I'm sorry. Can you say that again?	
Maria: The same disease spread out in China.	
Ms. H: Tell me more about that.	
Maria: Well, I think that because the same disease spread out in China, that they could have spread it to someone else.	
Ms. H: OK. And what evidence do we have that it was spread into Europe? Julio?	• Ms. Hatt reinforces the idea that she is asking students to identify evidence.
Julio: 'Cause when it arrived in [inaudible] that most of the people on it was dead already.	
Ms. H: Does anybody want to add on to that or say more about that? Carol, did you want to say more about that? Olivia?	
Olivia: Many of the ship's crewmen were sick.	
Ms. H: OK. If you go back into that paragraph on page 2, you'll see that the author actually mentions the word *evidence* in that first sentence. It says, "There is a convincing piece of evidence for this theory. It is an account of an eyewitness from Sicily." An account is a description of events. So we can gather information from people's descriptions of what they saw, right?	• When students do not pick up on the eyewitness account, Ms. Hatt directs them to the sentence in the text that mentions that account.
Ms. H: That happens even now in the news. Sometimes people are interviewed, and they tell their accounts of what happened, right? And so this person said that a fleet of ships arrived in Sicily in October 1347, and many of the ships' crewmen were already dead when the ships docked.	

Discussion Moves Demonstrated in the Video Episodes

We selected the video episodes that you viewed while reading this chapter to demonstrate the discussion moves summarized below.

- Video Episode 3.1: Scaffolding Student Thinking
  - Provide a concrete example of an abstract concept: The paper chain represents the causal chain.
  - Consistently make use of key terms (*causal chain, chain, link, links, events,* and *connect*) in eliciting student thinking.
  - Cue students to return to the text for important information.
- Video Episode 3.2: More Examples of Scaffolding
  - Provide explanation of the key term (*theory*) and display the explanation in writing: "theory: a working idea or explanation that takes into account the available information."
  - Consistently make use of key terms (*theory, explanation,* and *evidence*) in eliciting student thinking.
  - Cue students to return to the text for important information and model doing that.

Take It Away

Once again, we encourage you to make copies of "Black Death" and use the discussion plan for discussing it with your students. We also strongly recommend that you audiotape or videotape the discussion and transcribe key episodes. The transcripts will allow you to analyze your discussion moves and how students responded to them. You can also analyze students' exit activities to discover what they learned from the discussion.

Use the transcript analysis tools in Appendix A to guide your analysis.

CHAPTER 4

Planning and Discussing "Coral Reefs"

The focus of attention in this chapter is the text "Coral Reefs" by Joanna Solins. As in the two previous chapters, we describe our process of planning for a discussion of the text and present video episodes of the discussion enactment. However, in this chapter, we also show how our planning changed as a result of rereading the text and watching the videotapes of how the discussion of the text was enacted by Ms. Hatt and Mr. Weinberg.

Careful Reading of the Text

Read "Coral Reefs," which appears on the following pages, and take some notes about the text. Write on your copy of the text and use sticky notes to mark important parts. Think about what the text presents in terms of opportunities for students to learn about important content, useful text features, and disciplinary knowledge. Also consider any research that you might want to do to feel confident in discussing the text with students.

Coral Reefs

by Joanna Solins

Types of Coral Reefs

Fringing Reef

Barrier Reef

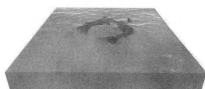

Coral Atoll

Dive down into clear tropical water, and you're likely to find a rich and beautiful ocean community. Rainbow-hued fish flit around complex structures in a wide array of shapes, sizes, and colors. Some look like brains, and others like fingers. Some look like deer antlers. Others sway fanlike in the ocean currents. You are looking at a coral reef.

Coral reefs are found in warm, shallow waters around the world, but especially in tropical areas along the coast and on the fringes of volcanic islands. Some coral reefs, called atolls, are ring-shaped. They form on top of underwater volcanoes.

From a distance, coral reefs can look like rocky underwater islands covered with plants. Get up close, though, and you'll find that the "rocks" are alive. Many of the "plants" are really animals. These structures are all created by tiny, simple animals called corals.

CORAL REEFS | 1

Corals are related to jellyfish. Their bodies are water-filled sacs. They have a mouth surrounded by stinging tentacles. Unlike jellyfish, though, adult corals do not move around. Instead, they build cup-shaped skeletons to protect their soft bodies. Reef-building corals live in large groups called colonies. A single colony can contain thousands of individual animals, called polyps.

Different species of coral grow in different patterns, forming the variety of shapes on the reef. The colonies grow larger as some polyps die off and leave their skeletons behind. New polyps then create skeletons on top of the old ones. Large reef-building colonies may grow less than one inch per year.

Coral polyps use their stinging tentacles to catch tiny organisms that float by. They have another important source of food, too, though. Coral polyps have algae living in their bodies. The algae can use the sun's light to create energy, just like plants. In return for nutrients and a safe place to live, the algae give the polyp oxygen and nutrients that it needs. Algae can provide a coral polyp with more than half of its energy. The algae also give the coral its beautiful colors. Most corals must live in shallow, clear water so that the algae can get enough sunlight.

Octocoral

Pink Coral

Elkhorn Coral

CORAL REEFS | 2

Coral reefs are important for many reasons. They support a huge diversity of life. Though they cover less than one percent of the ocean floor, they are home to about 25 percent of ocean species. That's more than a million different species! Humans rely on reefs, too. Reefs are home to fish that people eat. Reefs also protect beaches and coastal communities from pounding ocean waves during storms. They provide income for many people through the tourism they create.

Unfortunately, coral reefs are in danger. Careless divers, people who collect coral, and poor fishing practices all damage reefs directly. Pollution from coastal developments and fuel from boats are large problems, too. They can poison the coral and make the water cloudy. In cloudy water, the algae living in the coral can't get enough sunlight.

CORAL REEFS | 3

Coral Bleaching

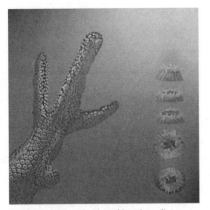

Healthy coral with plant-like algae living inside polyps

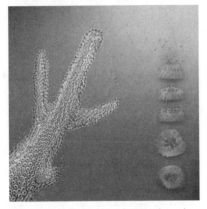

Bleached coral with algae being released from polyps

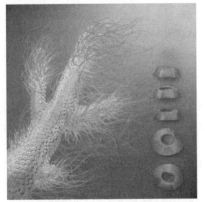

Dead coral skeleton covered with thread-like algae or plants growing on the outside

One of the biggest problems facing coral reefs today is called "coral bleaching." Under certain types of stress, corals can lose their algae. The term "bleaching" is used because corals appear white without algae. If conditions return to normal quickly, corals can replace algae and recover. Otherwise, they die.

Scientists do not understand coral bleaching very well yet. They know that warmer water temperatures cause corals to bleach, but they don't know why. One theory is that the warmer water stresses the coral. It produces fewer nutrients for the algae, so the algae leave. Another theory is that the warm water stresses the algae. The stressed algae produce less oxygen, and the coral releases them.

Whatever causes the algae to leave, though, there have been many more coral bleaching events in recent years. Many people believe that global warming is to blame. When humans burn fuel, gases are released into the atmosphere. These gases trap heat. Many scientists now agree that all of the heat-trapping gases in our atmosphere are causing the global temperature to rise. Even a small rise in temperature can cause bleaching, so global warming is a threat to corals.

People around the world are working to help coral reefs. You can, too. If you are lucky enough to visit a reef, make sure that you learn how to enjoy it without causing damage. Never take home a coral souvenir.

Even from home, you can make a difference. By conserving energy and reducing trash and pollution, you can improve the environment for coral reefs.

CORAL REEFS | 4

Reading the Text: Our Notes

Compare your notations with ours below.

Text	Our Notes
page 1	
Coral Reefs by Joanna Solins Dive down into clear tropical water, and you're likely to find a rich and beautiful ocean community. Rainbow-hued fish flit around complex structures in a wide array of shapes, sizes, and colors. Some look like brains, and others like fingers. Some look like deer antlers. Others sway fanlike in the ocean currents. You are looking at a coral reef. Coral reefs are found in warm, shallow waters around the world, but especially in tropical areas along the coast and on the fringes of volcanic islands. Some coral reefs, called atolls, are ring-shaped. They form on top of underwater volcanoes. From a distance, coral reefs can look like rocky underwater islands covered with plants. Get up close, though, and you'll find that the "rocks" are alive. Many of the "plants" are really animals. These structures are all created by tiny, simple animals called corals.	• The information needed to understand the features of a coral reef is provided across the six paragraphs on pages 1 and 2. • The first paragraph provides a poetic description of a coral reef. The photos are stunning, but they don't give a sense of the living coral reef that is being described. • All three paragraphs on page 1 provide many disconnected pieces of information but no clear explanation of what a coral reef is. Coral reefs are referred to in a variety of ways, none of which offer a complete representation. • The referents for coral reefs include "rich and beautiful ocean community," "complex structures," "atolls," "rocky underwater islands covered with plants," "'rocks' are alive," "'plants' are really animals," "these structures," and "tiny, simple animals called corals."
page 2	
Corals are related to jellyfish. Their bodies are water-filled sacs. They have a mouth surrounded by stinging tentacles. Unlike jellyfish, though, adult corals do not move around. Instead, they build cup-shaped skeletons to protect their soft bodies. Reef-building corals live in large groups called colonies. A single colony can contain thousands of individual animals, called polyps. Different species of coral grow in different patterns, forming the variety of shapes on the reef. The colonies grow larger as some polyps die off and leave their skeletons behind. New polyps then create skeletons on top of the old ones. Large reef-building colonies may grow less than one inch per year.	• The first two paragraphs provide important information: (a) A coral is an animal. (b) An individual coral is called a polyp. (c) A polyp has a soft body, which is really a water-filled sac. (d) A polyp has a mouth surrounded by stinging tentacles. (e) Polyps are related to jellyfish, which also have soft bodies and tentacles. (f) Adult polyps make a cup-shaped skeleton for protection. (g) Once they make the skeleton, they no longer move around (unlike jellyfish). (h) A coral reef is made up of thousands of polyps, which have built their skeletons on top of skeletons of polyps that have died. (i) A reef grows less than an inch a year. *(continued)*

Text	Our Notes
page 2 *continued*	
Coral polyps use their stinging tentacles to catch tiny organisms that float by. They have another important source of food, too, though. Coral polyps have algae living in their bodies. The algae can use the sun's light to create energy, just like plants. In return for nutrients and a safe place to live, the algae give the polyp oxygen and nutrients that it needs. Algae can provide a coral polyp with more than half of its energy. The algae also give the coral its beautiful colors. Most corals must live in shallow, clear water so that the algae can get enough sunlight.	• This paragraph provides important information about how coral secures its food: (a) catching tiny organisms with its tentacles, which connects to information in the first paragraph on this page ("mouth surrounded by stinging tentacles"). (b) Algae provide oxygen and nutrients. • The information about the algae and the coral reveals the interdependence of these two organisms. • The algae provide the coral polyp with nutrients (food) and oxygen. • The coral polyp provides the algae with a safe place to live and with nutrients. • The information about living in shallow, clear water in this paragraph connects to information in the second paragraph on page 1 ("Coral reefs are found in warm, shallow waters…").
page 3	
Coral reefs are important for many reasons. They support a huge diversity of life. Though they cover less than one percent of the ocean floor, they are home to about 25 percent of ocean species. That's more than a million different species! Humans rely on reefs, too. Reefs are home to fish that people eat. Reefs also protect beaches and coastal communities from pounding ocean waves during storms. They provide income for many people through the tourism they create.	• The two paragraphs on this page begin with topic sentences that cue readers to upcoming content. That is important for students to notice. • Coral reefs are important because they (a) support a huge diversity of life (ecosystem), (b) are home to fish that provide food, (c) protect beaches and communities from waves during storms, and (d) provide jobs related to tourism.
Unfortunately, coral reefs are in danger. Careless divers, people who collect coral, and poor fishing practices all damage reefs directly. Pollution from coastal developments and fuel from boats are large problems, too. They can poison the coral and make the water cloudy. In cloudy water, the algae living in the coral can't get enough sunlight.	• Coral reefs are in danger from (a) careless divers and people who collect coral, (b) fishing practices, and (c) pollution. • Pollution can make the water cloudy, and in cloudy water, algae can't get enough sunlight. • The information about the coral and sunlight in this paragraph connects to information on page 2 ("Most corals must live in shallow, clear water so that the algae can get enough sunlight."). *(continued)*

Text	Our Notes
page 4	
One of the biggest problems facing coral reefs today is called "coral bleaching." Under certain types of stress, corals can lose their algae. The term "bleaching" is used because corals appear white without algae. If conditions return to normal quickly, corals can replace algae and recover. Otherwise, they die.	• *Stress* means to upset the balance in the ecosystem, causing harm to polyps and algae. • *Bleaching* refers to whitening, or removing the color from something. • *Coral bleaching* refers to coral losing its algae. When the algae leave, coral look white. • Coral bleaching can lead to death for corals. • The illustration shows a progression from a healthy coral with algae inside to a dead coral skeleton with algae on the outside. It shows multiple views of a cross-section of the polyp—living, dying, and dead. The side view of the polyp cross-section is shifted downward so viewers can see the inside of the polyp.
Scientists do not understand coral bleaching very well yet. They know that warmer water temperatures cause corals to bleach, but they don't know why. One theory is that the warmer water stresses the coral. It produces fewer nutrients for the algae, so the algae leave. Another theory is that the warm water stresses the algae. The stressed algae produce less oxygen, and the coral releases them.	• The big idea here is that warmer water causes corals to bleach, but the specific way the bleaching occurs is not understood and cannot yet be explained by scientists. • Students need to understand that a theory is an explanation or an idea about why things happen. • Scientists develop theories by observing and describing what they see. Then, they use their observation and description to develop a causal chain, or organization of information into cause-and-effect links. The causal chain is a working theory. • Scientists have two theories about the causes of coral bleaching: (1) Warmer water stresses coral, so it produces fewer nutrients for the algae, causing the algae to leave. (2) Warmer water stresses algae, so it produces less oxygen for the coral and causes the coral to release them. *(continued)*

Text	Our Notes
page 4 continued	
Whatever causes the algae to leave, though, there have been many more coral bleaching events in recent years. Many people believe that global warming is to blame. When humans burn fuel, gases are released into the atmosphere. These gases trap heat. Many scientists now agree that all of the heat-trapping gases in our atmosphere are causing the global temperature to rise. Even a small rise in temperature can cause bleaching, so global warming is a threat to corals.	• People, including scientists, have a theory about what causes coral bleaching. • Global warming is an increase in the temperature of the Earth. • Many scientists agree that global warming is caused by gases released when fuel is burned. Those gases are released into the atmosphere. Those gases trap heat. The trapped heat warms up the atmosphere and raises the temperature on Earth.
People around the world are working to help coral reefs. You can, too. If you are lucky enough to visit a reef, make sure that you learn how to enjoy it without causing damage. Never take home a coral souvenir. Even from home, you can make a difference. By conserving energy and reducing trash and pollution, you can improve the environment for coral reefs.	• Articles about the environment often end with a note to readers about the role they can play in preserving it. • This is an opportunity to emphasize the interdependence of the coral reef ecosystem and the global ecosystem.

Analyzing "Coral Reefs"

Here again, we analyzed "Coral Reefs" by focusing on important content, useful text features, and opportunities to develop disciplinary knowledge.

Content

"Coral Reefs" provides an account of a specific ecosystem and presents a description of the interdependence of the organisms in that ecosystem. The text also describes how the coral reef ecosystem is related to the larger global ecosystem and how developments in the global ecosystem affect the coral reef ecosystem.

Ecosystem and *interdependence* are ideas that will allow students to organize the text information into a coherent mental representation, or situation model, rather than just a collection of interesting facts.

Research

We did some research to prepare ourselves for planning a discussion of "Coral Reefs":

• *Coral polyp/algae interdependence:* Because the important information in this text relates to the interdependence of the coral polyps and algae in the coral reef ecosystem, it is important to understand how the coral polyp and algae interact. Students need to understand that the algae are plants. Like other plants, the algae engage in photosynthesis. They use carbon dioxide and sunlight to create food (nutrients), which the coral can change into energy. The algae also take in carbon dioxide and release oxygen, which is what plants do. Human beings eat food (nutrients) and transform it into energy that their bodies use.

- *Global warming:* Historical temperature records provide evidence that the Earth's temperature is rising. Scientists point to the following causes for this:
  - Burning fossil fuels (gas, coal, oil) releases gases into the atmosphere. Carbon dioxide is one of these gases.
  - Carbon dioxide and other gases trap heat in the atmosphere.
  - Forests absorb much of the carbon dioxide in the atmosphere, but when forests are cut down, that carbon dioxide is not absorbed.

Students might think that global warming is caused by warm air rising as fuel is burned. It is the gases, particularly carbon dioxide, that are released during burning that trap heat in the atmosphere.

Text Features
The text provides opportunities for focusing on important language cues, paragraph conventions, and graphics.

- *Language cues:* The first page of the text provides multiple referents for the coral reef. Likewise, the first paragraph on page 2 provides multiple referents for the coral polyp. Students need to understand that there can be many referents that refer to one concept.
- *Paragraph conventions:* Paragraphs on the first two pages do not include conventional topic sentences, but paragraphs on the last two pages do.
- *Graphics:* The text is lavishly illustrated with photographs of a coral reef. The illustration on page 4 is particularly important because it shows the process of coral bleaching. But it is a complex representation that needs to be explained. The illustration shows the progression from a healthy coral with algae inside to a dead coral skeleton with algae on the outside. It shows multiple views of a cross-section of the polyp—living, dying, and dead. The side view of the polyp cross-section is shifted downward so viewers can see the inside of the polyp.

Disciplinary Knowledge
"Coral Reefs" provides an opportunity for students to learn about the work of scientists who develop theories based on their observations and descriptions. Developing a theory involves organizing information into causal chains to explain natural events.

Selecting Learning Goals
In the following table, we show our initial set of learning goals and the set that we developed after watching the lesson plan enacted in classrooms and analyzing the text in a more rigorous way using the content/text features/disciplinary knowledge framework. Compare our first set of goals (take 1) with our second set (take 2).

Take 1	Take 2
What is coral? Corals are animals called polyps. Polyps are soft-bodied creatures that create hard skeletons.	**What are the important features of the coral reef ecosystem?** Like other ecosystems, the plants and animals of a coral reef live and grow in a specific environment that provides food and protection.
What are coral reefs, and how are they formed? Coral reefs are made up of the skeletons of dead polyps on which new polyps have grown. These polyps have algae living in their bodies. Coral reefs are complex and sensitive ecosystems that provide an example of interdependence in nature: The coral polyps and the algae that live inside them are dependent on one another.	**In what ways are coral polyps and algae in a coral reef interdependent?** Plant algae live in the animal polyps of the coral reef. Like other plants, the algae use photosynthesis to create food, or nutrients. In the process of photosynthesis, carbon dioxide is taken in, and oxygen is released. The polyps use the food and oxygen provided by the algae. In turn, the polyps provide nutrients and protection for the algae.
What has the study of coral reefs revealed about our environment? The study reveals in specific ways how changes brought about by pollution and global warming affect the coral reef ecosystem.	**In what ways is the coral reef ecosystem interdependent with other ecosystems?** The coral reef ecosystem is affected by the global ecosystem, which is changing because of global warming.
There are many phenomena in the world that scientists are still trying to explain. The death of coral reefs (coral bleaching) is one example.	**What theories are scientists investigating to explain the causal chain related to coral bleaching?** Scientists have two theories to explain coral bleaching. Both theories are presented in the form of a causal chain. The chain explains how global warming creates warmer water: (1) The warm water stresses the polyps, so they produce fewer nutrients for the algae, causing the algae to leave. (2) The warm water stresses the algae, so they produce less oxygen for the polyps, causing the polyps to release the algae.

We see our initial learning goals (take 1) as being focused on important text information but without explicit reference to how those ideas might be organized into a coherent mental representation, or situation model. The second set of goals (take 2) makes the important organizing ideas of ecosystem and interdependence, and theory and causal chain much more obvious.

Take 1	Take 2 (These goals did not change.)
How can graphics support readers in understanding the text more deeply? The diagram on page 4 is integral to understanding the process of coral bleaching described in the text.	**How can graphics support readers in understanding the text more deeply?** The diagram on page 4 is integral to understanding the process of coral bleaching described in the text.

Designing the Exit

We created several versions of an exit for a discussion of "Coral Reefs." We kept in mind not only the learning goals but also the need to keep the activity short enough to complete after the discussion.

As you can see by reading the versions below, the language in our exit became more precise and focused on the most important aspects of the situation model in the text.

- *Take 1:* Provide the students the following word bank: *coral polyps, algae, coral bleaching,* and *global warming.* Ask students to write three sentences using these words to explain what they have learned.
- *Take 2:* How are coral polyps, algae, coral bleaching, and global warming related?
- *Take 3:* Explain how coral polyps, algae, coral bleaching, and global warming are related.
- *Take 4:* Explain the interdependence in a coral reef ecosystem using what you have learned about coral polyps, algae, coral bleaching, and global warming.

We think the final version comes closest to eliciting a situation model from students.

Designing the Launch

We had an initial plan for a launch and then revised it based on what we saw when Ms. Hatt and Mr. Weinberg used it with students.

Take 1

In the initial plan, we suggested teachers display a piece of coral skeleton, which is white. The skeleton was the only representation students had of coral. We can only imagine their confusion when the teacher began reading about the colorful shapes in the coral reef.

We also suggested that students look at the pictures in the article, but based on what students talked about when they did so, we saw that their comments were limited to pointing out interesting shapes and colors.

Take 2

To give students a sense of the living coral reef as an ecosystem, we searched online for "YouTube coral reef" and "YouTube jellyfish" and found several YouTube videos that could serve as a launch for the text. Using the videos as a launch might be particularly appropriate for English learners.

Showing the video clips will only take a few minutes, but it will provide a memorable representation of what students will learn about as well as a reference point as students read about coral reefs.

Before showing the video clips, we would say something like this:

Today we're going to read about coral reefs. We'll also read about jellyfish. Take a look at these videos to see what a coral reef and jellyfish look like.

Designing the Discussion Plan

In the section that follows, we show how our text analysis and research and the learning goals informed a discussion plan for "Coral Reefs." The plan is not a script but an example of how a discussion plan can support student comprehension.

Discussion Plan for "Coral Reefs"

Learning Goals

1. What are the important features of the coral reef ecosystem?

   Like other ecosystems, the plants and animals of a coral reef live and grow in a specific environment that provides food and protection.

Coral Reef Ecosystem

Environment	Food	Protection	Growth
• Warm, shallow water • Especially in tropical areas near the coast • On the fringes of volcanic islands • Clear water	• Coral polyps catch food with their tentacles. • Algae inside the coral polyps produce food for the polyps. • The polyps produce food for the algae, too.	• Coral polyps have soft bodies, so they build skeletons.	• Coral polyps build their skeletons on top of old skeletons, building up the coral reef.

2. In what ways are coral polyps and algae in a coral reef interdependent?

   Plant algae live in the animal polyps of the coral reef. Like other plants, the algae use photosynthesis to create food, or nutrients. In the process of photosynthesis, carbon dioxide is taken in, and oxygen is released. The polyps use the food and oxygen provided by the algae. In turn, the polyps provide nutrients and protection for the algae.

3. In what ways is the coral reef ecosystem interdependent with other ecosystems?

   The coral reef ecosystem is affected by the global ecosystem, which is changing because of global warming.

   Fossil fuels → Global warming:

   People burn fossil fuels.

   ↓

   Gases are released into the atmosphere.

   ↓

   Gases trap heat.

   ↓

   Global temperatures rise.

   ↓

   Water gets warmer.

4. What theories are scientists investigating to explain the causal chain related to coral bleaching?

   Scientists have two theories to explain coral bleaching. Both theories are presented in the form of a causal chain:

   (1) In one theory, the warm water stresses the polyps, so they produce fewer nutrients for the algae, and the algae leave.

   (2) In another theory, the warm water stresses the algae, so they produce less oxygen for the polyps, and the polyps release the algae.

Warmer Water → Coral Bleaching

Theory 1	Theory 2
Warm water stresses coral.	Warm water stresses algae.
↓	↓
Stressed coral produces fewer nutrients for algae.	Stressed algae produce less oxygen.
↓	↓
Algae leave.	Coral releases algae.
↓	↓
Coral bleaching	Coral bleaching

5. How can graphics support readers in understanding the text more deeply?

The diagram on page 4 is integral to understanding the process of coral bleaching described in the text.

Resources

- Copies of "Coral Reefs"
- YouTube video clips of a coral reef and jellyfish
- Chart paper with *Coral Reef Ecosystem* as the main heading and *Environment*, *Food*, *Protection*, and *Growth* as column headings
- Chart paper and markers
- White and green crayons or colored pencils (if you are using the black-and-white version of the text)
- Task sheets with the exit prompt:

  Explain the interdependence in a coral reef ecosystem using what you learned about coral polyps, algae, coral bleaching, and global warming.

Launch

Before showing video clips of a coral reef and jellyfish, say:

Today we're going to read an informational article about coral reefs. We'll also read about jellyfish. Take a look at these videos to see what a coral reef and jellyfish look like.

The **bolded** text in the following table provides instructions for what you should do. Instructions to read, for example, mean that you or a volunteer should read the indicated text aloud.

Text	Our Notes	Reader–Text Interactions
page 1		
Coral Reefs by Joanna Solins Dive down into clear tropical water, and you're likely to find a rich and beautiful ocean community. Rainbow-hued fish flit around complex structures in a wide array of shapes, sizes, and colors. Some look like brains, and others like fingers. Some look like deer antlers. Others sway fanlike in the ocean currents. You are looking at a coral reef. Coral reefs are found in warm, shallow waters around the world, but especially in tropical areas along the coast and on the fringes of volcanic islands. Some coral reefs, called atolls, are ring-shaped. They form on top of underwater volcanoes. From a distance, coral reefs can look like rocky underwater islands covered with plants. Get up close, though, and you'll find that the "rocks" are alive. Many of the "plants" are really animals. These structures are all created by tiny, simple animals called corals.	• The information needed to understand the features of a coral reef is provided across the six paragraphs on pages 1 and 2. • The first paragraph provides a poetic description of a coral reef. The photos are stunning, but they don't give a sense of the living coral reef that is being described. • All three paragraphs on page 1 provide many disconnected pieces of information but no clear explanation of what a coral reef is. Coral reefs are referred to in a variety of ways, none of which offer a complete representation. • The referents for coral reefs include "rich and beautiful ocean community," "complex structures," "atolls," "rocky underwater islands covered with plants," "'rocks' are alive," "'plants' are really animals," "these structures," and "tiny, simple animals called corals."	• **After viewing the video clips, distribute copies of "Coral Reefs."** • **Read the title and author.** • *Take a few moments to look at the photographs in this article entitled "Coral Reefs." What do you see that connects to what you saw in the video?* • **Read all three paragraphs.** • *The paragraphs on this first page include many words and phrases that refer to a coral reef. For example, in the first paragraph, the author mentions "a rich and beautiful ocean community."* • *What other words and phrases describe this community?* • *We have many words and phrases to describe the coral reef, but we still don't have a clear idea of what it really is.* • *Let's read on.* *(continued)*

Text	Our Notes	Reader–Text Interactions
page 2		
Corals are related to jellyfish. Their bodies are water-filled sacs. They have a mouth surrounded by stinging tentacles. Unlike jellyfish, though, adult corals do not move around. Instead, they build cup-shaped skeletons to protect their soft bodies. Reef-building corals live in large groups called colonies. A single colony can contain thousands of individual animals, called polyps. Different species of coral grow in different patterns, forming the variety of shapes on the reef. The colonies grow larger as some polyps die off and leave their skeletons behind. New polyps then create skeletons on top of the old ones. Large reef-building colonies may grow less than one inch per year.	• The first two paragraphs provide important information: (a) A coral is an animal. (b) An individual coral is called a polyp. (c) A polyp has a soft body, which is really a water-filled sac. (d) A polyp has a mouth surrounded by stinging tentacles. (e) Polyps are related to jellyfish, which also have soft bodies and tentacles. (f) Adult polyps make a cup-shaped skeleton for protection. (g) Once they make the skeleton, they no longer move around (unlike jellyfish). (h) A coral reef is made up of thousands of polyps, which have built their skeletons on top of skeletons of polyps that have died. (i) A reef grows less than an inch a year.	• **Read the first paragraph.** • *In this paragraph, we read about corals, adult corals, reef-building corals, colonies, and polyps. Let's sort this out.* • *What is a coral polyp?* • *How is a polyp like a jellyfish?* • *How is a polyp different from a jellyfish?* • *Let's see if we can use our hands to represent what the author is describing here. First, think about a single polyp in its cup-shaped skeleton.* • *Now, think about a polyp that has died and left behind its skeleton and what a new polyp does when it builds its skeleton.* • **(Or you may want to have students draw these representations on the board.)**
		• *The information that we've been reading describes the coral reef ecosystem. An ecosystem is a community of organisms and their environment.* • *What other ecosystems do you know?* • *Let's use this table to organize the information that we're reading.* • **Have students provide information from pages 1 and 2 to complete the table as follows.**

Coral Reef Ecosystem

Environment	Food	Protection	Growth
• Warm, shallow water • Especially in tropical areas near the coast • On the fringes of volcanic islands • Clear water	• Coral polyps catch food with their tentacles. • Algae inside the coral polyps produce food for the polyps. • The polyps produce food for the algae, too.	• Coral polyps have soft bodies, so they build skeletons.	• Coral polyps build their skeletons on top of old skeletons, building up the coral reef.

(continued)

Text	Our Notes	Reader–Text Interactions
page 2 *continued*		
Coral polyps use their stinging tentacles to catch tiny organisms that float by. They have another important source of food, too, though. Coral polyps have algae living in their bodies. The algae can use the sun's light to create energy, just like plants. In return for nutrients and a safe place to live, the algae give the polyp oxygen and nutrients that it needs. Algae can provide a coral polyp with more than half of its energy. The algae also give the coral its beautiful colors. Most corals must live in shallow, clear water so that the algae can get enough sunlight.	• This paragraph provides important information about how coral secures its food: (a) catching tiny organisms with its tentacles, which connects to information in the first paragraph on this page ("mouth surrounded by stinging tentacles"). (b) Algae provide oxygen and nutrients. • The information about the algae and the coral reveals the interdependence of these two organisms. • The algae provide the coral polyp with nutrients (food) and oxygen. • The coral polyp provides the algae with a safe place to live and with nutrients. • The information about living in shallow, clear water in this paragraph connects to information in the second paragraph on page 1 ("Coral reefs are found in warm, shallow waters…").	• **Read the next paragraph.** • *The author doesn't use the word* interdependence, *but that's what this paragraph is all about. The algae and the coral polyps are interdependent. They depend on each other.* • *Remember that the polyp is an animal. It says here that algae are like plants.* • *How do plants make food?* • *What does the algae provide for the polyps?* • *What do the polyps provide for the algae?* • *Let's add information to the table, including the information about the clear, shallow water. We read about the shallow water earlier. Here we find out about it being clear.* *(continued)*

Text	Our Notes	Reader–Text Interactions
page 3		
Coral reefs are important for many reasons. They support a huge diversity of life. Though they cover less than one percent of the ocean floor, they are home to about 25 percent of ocean species. That's more than a million different species! Humans rely on reefs, too. Reefs are home to fish that people eat. Reefs also protect beaches and coastal communities from pounding ocean waves during storms. They provide income for many people through the tourism they create. Unfortunately, coral reefs are in danger. Careless divers, people who collect coral, and poor fishing practices all damage reefs directly. Pollution from coastal developments and fuel from boats are large problems, too. They can poison the coral and make the water cloudy. In cloudy water, the algae living in the coral can't get enough sunlight.	• The two paragraphs on this page begin with topic sentences that cue readers to upcoming content. That is important for students to notice. • Coral reefs are important because they (a) support a huge diversity of life (ecosystem), (b) are home to fish that provide food, (c) protect beaches and communities from waves during storms, and (d) provide jobs related to tourism. • Coral reefs are in danger from (a) careless divers and people who collect coral, (b) fishing practices, and (c) pollution. • Pollution can make the water cloudy, and in cloudy water, algae can't get enough sunlight. • The information about the coral and sunlight in this paragraph connects to information on page 2 ("Most corals must live in shallow, clear water so that the algae can get enough sunlight.").	*This paragraph begins with a topic sentence. That sentence sets us up to know what we will read about. What will that be?* • **Read the paragraph.** • *Why are coral reefs important?* • *What does the author mean by the sentence "They support a huge diversity of life"?* • *The next paragraph also begins with a topic sentence. What will the paragraph be about?* • **Read the second paragraph.** • *What are dangers to coral reefs?* • *Why is pollution so harmful to the interdependence of the polyps and algae?* *(continued)*

Text	Our Notes	Reader–Text Interactions
page 4		
One of the biggest problems facing coral reefs today is called "coral bleaching." Under certain types of stress, corals can lose their algae. The term "bleaching" is used because corals appear white without algae. If conditions return to normal quickly, corals can replace algae and recover. Otherwise, they die.	• *Stress* means to upset the balance in the ecosystem, causing harm to polyps and algae. • *Bleaching* refers to whitening, or removing the color from something. • *Coral bleaching* refers to coral losing its algae. When the algae leave, coral look white. • Coral bleaching can lead to death for corals. • The illustration shows a progression from a healthy coral with algae inside to a dead coral skeleton with algae on the outside. It shows multiple views of a cross-section of the polyp—living, dying, and dead. The side view of the polyp cross-section is shifted downward so viewers can see the inside of the polyp.	• **Read the first sentence.** • *What is bleaching? What happens when you bleach something?* • **Read the rest of the paragraph.** • *In this paragraph, the word* stress *means to upset the balance in the ecosystem, causing harm to polyps and algae.* • *What happens when the coral reefs are stressed? Use the illustrations and captions on this page to explain what happens during coral bleaching.* • **Explain how the illustration should be "read."** • **If you are using the black-and-white version of the text, have students use the green and white crayons or pencils to color the illustration based on the information in the text and captions.** *(continued)*

Text	Our Notes	Reader–Text Interactions
page 4 *continued*		

Scientists do not understand coral bleaching very well yet. They know that warmer water temperatures cause corals to bleach, but they don't know why. One theory is that the warmer water stresses the coral. It produces fewer nutrients for the algae, so the algae leave. Another theory is that the warm water stresses the algae. The stressed algae produce less oxygen, and the coral releases them.	• The big idea here is that warmer water causes corals to bleach, but the specific way the bleaching occurs is not understood and cannot yet be explained by scientists.
	• Students need to understand that a theory is an explanation or an idea about why things happen.
	• Scientists develop theories by observing and describing what they see. Then, they use their observation and description to develop a causal chain, or organization of information into cause-and-effect links. The causal chain is a working theory.
	• Scientists have two theories about the causes of coral bleaching: (1) Warmer water stresses coral, so it produces fewer nutrients for the algae, causing the algae to leave. (2) Warmer water stresses algae, so it produces less oxygen for the coral and causes the coral to release them.
		• **Read the paragraph.**
		• *In this paragraph, the author explains how scientists are trying to understand coral bleaching by developing theories, or explanations.*
		• *Scientists develop theories by observing and describing what they see. Then, they use their observation and description to develop a causal chain, or organization of information into cause-and-effect links. The causal chain is a theory about what causes coral bleaching.*
		• *At this point, scientists have two theories to explain coral bleaching. They do not have evidence to support one theory over the other.*
		• *What are the two theories that scientists have about the cause of coral bleaching?*
		• **Have students contribute to creating the causal chains as a whole group, or have students work in small groups:**
		Warmer water → Coral bleaching
		    Theory 1
		    Theory 2
		Fossil fuels → Global warming

Whatever causes the algae to leave, though, there have been many more coral bleaching events in recent years. Many people believe that global warming is to blame. When humans burn fuel, gases are released into the atmosphere. These gases trap heat. Many scientists now agree that all of the heat-trapping gases in our atmosphere are causing the global temperature to rise. Even a small rise in temperature can cause bleaching, so global warming is a threat to corals.	• People, including scientists, have a theory about what causes coral bleaching. • Global warming is an increase in the temperature of the Earth. • Many scientists agree that global warming is caused by gases released when fuel is burned. Those gases are released into the atmosphere. Those gases trap heat. The trapped heat warms up the atmosphere and raises the temperature on Earth.	• **Read the paragraph.** • *In this paragraph, we learn about another causal chain: events linking fossil fuels and global warming. Let's create the causal chains that are described here.* • **Engage students in explaining their causal chains.** *(continued)*

Comprehension Instruction Through Text-Based Discussion

Text	Our Notes	Reader–Text Interactions
page 4 *continued*		
People around the world are working to help coral reefs. You can, too. If you are lucky enough to visit a reef, make sure that you learn how to enjoy it without causing damage. Never take home a coral souvenir.	• Articles about the environment often end with a note to readers about the role they can play in preserving it.	• **Read the last two paragraphs.** • *How does the information in this paragraph connect to the causal chains?* • *How is the coral reef ecosystem interdependent with the global ecosystem?*
Even from home, you can make a difference. By conserving energy and reducing trash and pollution, you can improve the environment for coral reefs.	• This is an opportunity to emphasize the interdependence of the coral reef ecosystem and the global ecosystem.	

Exit

Distribute the following task:

> Explain the interdependence in a coral reef ecosystem using what you learned about coral polyps, algae, coral bleaching, and global warming.

Some Important Moves in the Discussion Plan

Some important moves in the "Coral Reefs" discussion plan include:

- *Imposing coherence on text information by focusing on important concepts:* Drawing students' attention to the coral reef as an ecosystem and the interdependence of the coral polyps and the algae as well as the interdependence of the coral reef ecosystem and the global ecosystem is a critical move in the discussion plan. The concepts of an ecosystem and interdependence support students in constructing a coherent mental representation of the detailed text information.

- *Scaffolding student understanding of important ideas:* The suggestion to have students represent the cup-shaped skeletons of the adult coral polyps through gestures or drawing came from our viewing of the discussions with Ms. Hatt and Mr. Weinberg and their students. Understanding the connection between the building of skeletons and the formation of a coral reef is complex but essential to understanding the coral reef ecosystem.

Viewing Video Episodes

The video episodes for this chapter feature both Ms. Hatt and Mr. Weinberg.

Video Episode 4.1: Clear Cues

As you watch this video episode, notice how Ms. Hatt provides clear cues to students about her thinking about the text and their thinking about it. Take notes about what you observe as you view this episode and then compare them with our notes in the table below.

 **4.1: Clear Cues (3:19)**

Video Episode 4.1: Clear Cues	Our Notes
Ms. H: We're on the second paragraph where it says "coral reefs." Find that paragraph and follow along. [reading] "Coral reefs are found in warm, shallow waters around the world, but especially in tropical areas along the coast and on the fringes of volcanic islands. Some coral reefs, called atolls, are ring-shaped. They form on top of underwater volcanoes."	• Ms. Hatt provides a clear cue to students about where they should be in the text.
Ms. H: Before we move on, I just glanced over to the side and noticed that the graphic feature that's on the left gives me more information about coral atoll, so I'm gonna take a moment to look at it. This is giving me more information about what I just read. All right.	• Here, Ms. Hatt gives students a clear cue about the graphic in the text that she notices and why the graphic is useful: "This is giving me more information about what I just read."
Ms. H [reading]: "From a distance, coral reefs can look like rocky underwater islands covered with plants. Get up close, though, and you'll find out that the 'rocks' are alive. Many of the 'plants' are really animals. These structures are all created by tiny, simple animals called corals."	
Student: Shawn was right.	
Student: Yeah.	*(continued)*

Video Episode 4.1: Clear Cues *continued*	Our Notes
Ms. H: Before we move on— Let's stay on this page, Eli. Before we move on, I want to do some talking. I want us to do some talking. I noticed that that first paragraph had a really poetic description of coral. Let me show you an example. The author wrote, "Others sway fanlike in the ocean currents." They also compared the coral to brains and fingers and deer antlers. The next two paragraphs that we just read, they were a little bit different. These two paragraphs give us specific information about corals. What was that information? What was that information that we just got from the author about corals? It was less poetic, more specific. What did you learn from those two paragraphs? I'll give you a little bit of thinking time. If you're not sure, go ahead and reread those two paragraphs. What information did you learn? Arianna?	• Ms. Hatt provides an example of the poetic description that she refers to. She contrasts that kind of description to the description offered in the next two paragraphs.
Arianna: I learned that coral, when it's like under the water, you—when you're far away, it could look like it's just a rock, and when you get up close, you can actually see that it's really an animal.	
Ms. H: Does anybody have anything more to add? Mary?	
Mary: That coral reefs are found in warm, shallow waters across the wo—around the world.	
Ms. H: Mary, that's an important idea. Let's remember that.	• Here, Ms. Hatt acknowledges Mary's comment and labels it as important.
Aveeni: I, I saw two things from both of the paragraphs. The first paragraph and the whole page was that they are a complex structure in a wide area of shapes, sizes, and colors. And then in the second paragraph, I noticed that they said something about the coast and long—and on the fringes of volcanic islands.	
Ms. H: OK. So, Aveeni, I noticed that you went back into that first paragraph that I mentioned had more of a poetic description, and you actually found some specific information that was hidden in there, right?	• Ms. Hatt acknowledges Aveeni's response and describes what Aveeni did to locate the valuable information that she identified.

Video Episode 4.2: Providing Frameworks for Thinking About Text Information

As you watch this video episode, notice how Ms. Hatt provides frameworks for students to organize their thinking about text information. Take notes about what you notice as you view this episode and then compare your notes with ours.

⊙ **4.2: Providing Frameworks for Thinking About Text Information (5:00)**

Video Episode 4.2: Providing Frameworks for Thinking About Text Information	Our Notes
Ms. H: So we know that this article is about a very specific kind of ecosystem. An ecosystem is a community of organisms that interact with their physical environment. So basically an ecosystem is nonliving and living stuff interacting. OK? We're talking about the coral reef ecosystem today. So there's certain types of information that we can expect to find in this article, and I've sort of put them here on this chart for you. We can expect to find information about the environment, right, which is the surroundings and the conditions that the organisms live in. We can expect to find out how they get their food, how they protect themselves, and how they grow.	• Ms. Hatt provides a framework for students to organize their thinking about the information about the coral reef on pages 1 and 2. She introduces the term *ecosystem* and displays a table with the features of an ecosystem. She will use that table to capture and organize the information that students will provide.
Ms. H: OK? So we're gonna be looking out for this information, and a little further on, we're going to actually be putting it down on this chart. Now we can move on. Let's flip the page. [reading] "Corals are related t—" Oh, Kaleel, let's move on. We're on page 2. [reading] "Corals are related to jellyfish. Their bodies are water-filled sacs. They have a mouth surrounded by stinging tentacles. Unlike jellyfish, though, adult corals do not move around. Instead, they build cup-shaped skeletons to protect their soft bodies." Here the author just informed us about corals by comparing and contrasting them to an animal we might be more familiar with, jellyfish. Did you find out how jellyfish and coral are similar? Let me know. What did the text say about how jellyfish and coral are similar? Nick?	• Here, Ms. Hatt provides a framework for students to organize their thinking about jellyfish and corals: comparing and contrasting, noting similarities and differences.
Nick: That they both are water-filled sacs with stinging tentacles.	
Ms. H: OK. Is that what you were gonna say, Gerald? Do you want to add on anything to that? OK. Aveeni?	*(continued)*

Video Episode 4.2: Providing Frameworks for Thinking About Text Information *continued*	**Our Notes**
Aveeni: I can tell how jellyfish and corals are alike because I can see when I see jellyfish, they're really soft. I can tell they're soft. They're kind of soft as a pillow but not as soft as a pillow. And how they're probably related to is—I see they have something flowing out around them, not their—but not, but not their skin. It's—	
Ms. H: Do you think those might be tentacles?	
Aveeni: Yeah. And then the corals, how they're related, they're probably inside— If you touch it really soft like as it might be as soft as a cookie that breaks up into little pieces really quick. That's probably how a coral feels without the skeleton.	
Ms. H: Hmm. It says here it's more like a water-filled sac, so maybe not as crumbly as cookies. But I see how you're, you're making that connection there.	
Ms. H: OK. So how are they different? What makes them different than coral? Darrell?	• Ms. Hatt returns to the compare/contrast framework by focusing students' attention on differences between jellyfish and coral. Both Darrell and McKenna use the framework in responding.
Darrell: What makes jellyfish different than coral, coral?	
Ms. H: Or coral different than jellyfish, however you want to word it.	
Darrell: They said that when coral, coral is an adult, it doesn't move around [inaudible] like jellyfish.	
Ms. H: Hmm. Anybody else want to add to that? McKenna?	
McKenna: To add to Darrell's, jellyfish, when they're an adult, they can move around, but coral, when they're an adult, they can't.	
Ms. H: OK. Somebody tell me more about that not being able to move around. What does that actually mean? Maria?	• Here, Ms. Hatt presses students to think about what Darrell and McKenna have said about the coral polyps not being able to move around, and Maria provides a clear explanation.
Maria: Because they can't move around because they build a skeleton around them, so like a shell with protection, so they really can't move around after that.	
Ms. H: Hmm, OK. Mary?	• Ms. Hatt presses Mary to be clear about how the jellyfish protection differs from the polyps' protection.
Mary: Like a jellyfish, there's a [inaudible] they have— I think for protection, they have like this big dome on top of them that—but it's—it's like— To me it's in a way protection, but it's really—but that's the safe part of them.	
Ms. H: But do you think it's still soft, or do you think it's hard?	
Mary: It's prob— Yeah, it's probably still soft.	*(continued)*

Video Episode 4.2: Providing Frameworks for Thinking About Text Information *continued*	Our Notes
Ms. H: And Nick, and then we'll move on to the next paragraph. Nick: [Inaudible] how jellyfish and coral are, aren't alike, but that jellyfish don't really form colo—they don't form colonies, but coral does. Ms. H: Hmm. Did you read somewhere that jellyfish don't form colonies? Nick: I just know that. Ms. H: Oh, you just know that. OK. 'Cause it wasn't in the text, and I don't—I actually don't know as much about jellyfish as you guys seem to, so I might have to look that up.	

Video Episodes 4.3.1 and 4.3.2: Grappling With Important Ideas

We selected two video episodes for you to watch this time. The first episode involves Ms. Hatt and her students grappling with several important ideas. The second episode involves Mr. Weinberg and his students grappling with the same ideas. As you watch these video episodes, compare how they unfolded. Jot down your observations and then compare them with ours.

 4.3.1: Grappling With Important Ideas: Ms. Hatt (5:41)

Video Episode 4.3.1: Grappling With Important Ideas: Ms. Hatt	Our Notes
Ms. H: Sure. What information did you find? Student: That the, the coral gives it [inaudible]. It forms the skeleton that cup so [inaudible]. Ms. H: OK, where would you—where should we put that? Student: Protection. Ms. H: OK. So the way that coral protects themselves is with cup-shaped skeletons. Is that what you meant? OK. Shawn, anything else? Shawn: The [inaudible] food they eat is tiny, tiny coral. When they're like sort of babies, they snatch food that—like little fish and other little creatures to eat. Ms. H: OK. So they catch food floating by. OK. Do you think they do that as adults as well? Shawn: Yeah. Ms. H: OK. Aveeni, you seem excited about something. Aveeni: When they grow up, up—this would be in Growth—adults don't move as much as babies do, as the, the little, the little—as the little, little coral grows. [Inaudible] That's supposed to be in Growth.	• There is important interrelated information in the text about the coral polyps' growth, their protection, and how they secure food. In this episode, Ms. Hatt and her students grapple with this information. • A student offers information to write under the Protection column in the ecosystem table, and Ms. Hatt revoices that information: Polyps form cup-shaped skeletons. • Shawn introduces the idea of how the polyps get their food when they are babies—by snatching little fish. • Ms. Hatt asks if that approach is used by adults, and Shawn agrees. • Aveeni points out that adult polyps don't move.

(continued)

Video Episode 4.3.1: Grappling With Important Ideas: Ms. Hatt *continued*	Our Notes
Ms. H: Oh, I'm sorry. Say that again. Aveeni: That when they're adults—that when they're adults, they don't move. They don't really move as much when they grow up. Ms. H: Mm-hmm. OK. So let's—before we write that down, let's talk more about that. Does anybody have some more information to add to Aveeni's about the growth of coral? Kaleel? Kaleel: That it can grow up to the top of the sea, and that can take 100 years. Ms. H: OK. So they, they do grow, right? And that—are you trying to say that they grow slowly or rapidly? Kaleel: Slowly. Ms. H: OK. Did they say one inch per year? Student: No, less than one inch. Ms. H: Less than one inch per year. OK. Mary? Mary: That they— To add to Aveeni's, I actually think it like [inaudible] well 'cause it say that they have these tentacles that grab little fishies that eat because at the—if they didn't move at all, there's just a little bit moving [inaudible]. Ms. H: So what part of the coral were you talking about when you said that they didn't move? Mary: When they, when they're adults. Ms. H: So which part of the coral, the soft sac or the skeleton? Mary: The soft sac. Ms. H: Those don't move, or are you talking about the coral, like th— Mary: No, I just mean like there's—that they said. Ms. H: OK. Let's go back into the text. Can you find that part for me? Mary: I think it was— Student: Yeah. Ms. H: Read it for us, Aveeni, if you wouldn't mind. We're on page 2, right? Aveeni: Yes. [reading] "Corals are related to jellyfish. Their bodies are water-filled sacs. They have a mouth surrounded by stinging tentacles. Unlike jellyfish, though—unlike jellyfish, though, adult corals do not move around. Instead, they build cup-shaped skeletons to protect their soft bodies. Reef—reef-building corals live in large groups called colonies. A single colony can contain thousands of individual animals called polyps."	• Ms. Hatt asks for more information about the growth of coral [reefs]. • Kaleel picks up on the growth idea and says that it takes a long time. • There are several important ideas on the table here: the growth of polyps and the formation of skeletons; the effect of the skeletons on polyps' movement and how they get food; and the growth of coral reefs, which involves polyps building their skeletons on top of the skeletons left by dead polyps. • Ms. Hatt asks students to return to the text to sort things out. *(continued)*

Video Episode 4.3.1: Grappling With Important Ideas: Ms. Hatt *continued*	Our Notes
Ms. H: Mm-hmm. Oh, actually, you know what? Now that, now that you were reading, why don't you continue reading because I see in the first sentence of that second paragraph, I see the word *grow*. So that interests me because we were talking about growth. Aveeni: [reading] "Different species of coral grow in different patterns, forming the variety of shapes on the reef. The colonies grow larger as, as some polyps die off and leave their skeletons behind." Ms. H: OK. So tell me a little bit about their growth. What did you just learn? Anybody. Aveeni: Sometimes they— Ms. H: Oh. Go ahead. Aveeni: —leave behind their skeletons while they grow. Ms. H: OK. So new polyps— Finish the sentence for me, Aveeni. New polyps grow on top of— Aveeni: Grow on top—that's not really what I said, but I said— Well, it's kind of what I said, but I don't think it's exactly what I said. I said that it grows out—it lets its—the skeleton behind while it grows. Ms. H: Ah, OK. So I reworded it a little bit, but I think I'm saying the same thing that you said. That it's growing, right? New polyps and they're growing on top of the skeletons that are left behind, right? OK.	• At this point, Ms. Hatt tries to organize the information that students are providing by using the ecosystem table.

 4.3.2: Grappling With Important Ideas: Mr. Weinberg (2:46)

Video Episode 4.3.2: Grappling With Important Ideas: Mr. Weinberg	Our Notes
Mr. W: OK. Let's read at the top, top of page 2. [reading] "Corals are related to jellyfish. Their bodies are water-filled sacs. They have a mouth surrounded by stinging tentacles. Unlike jellyfish, though, adult corals do not move around. Instead, th— instead, they build cup-shaped skeletons to protect their soft bodies. Reef-building corals live in large groups called colonies. A single colony can contain thousands of indi—individual animals, called polyps." Did anyone hear a way that they protect themselves in that paragraph, 'cause we should add it to our chart about ecosystems over here. Ashton, what'd you hear?	• In this episode, Mr. Weinberg and his students grapple with the same ideas that Ms. Hatt and her students were trying to understand. • Both teachers are using the table to organize the information about the coral reef ecosystem.

(continued)

Video Episode 4.3.2: Grappling With Important Ideas: Mr. Weinberg *continued*	**Our Notes**
Ashton: They have a sting coral. Mr. W: Say again a little louder. Ashton: They have corals to protect them. Mr. W: They have corals to protect. Well, we're talking about corals. Read the part that you're talking about. Ashton: I think it was talking about like the mouths are surrounded by stinging tentacles. Mr. W: Stinging tentacles? Ashton: Yeah. Mr. W: OK. So for protection— Well, here we've got stinging te— Tentacles catch organisms, but they also protect themselves, right, the stinging tentacles. Did anyone no—notice anything about the cup-shaped something in that paragraph right there? What'd you notice, Jeannette? Jeannette: It's always— [reading] "Instead they build cup-shaped skeletons to protect their soft bodies." Mr. W: What do you think that does, a cup-shaped skeleton? Why would that be a form of protection? Student: So that when someone tries to eat them when they swim to a cup shape, that will help, help them protect themselves. Mr. W: Does that make it harder for an enemy to, to get to them? 'Cause it's like a, it's like a cup, right? Go ahead, Haley. Haley: That they build hard shells around their soft bodies to protect them. Mr. W: Thanks. OK. They have hard shells around their bodies. And why are hard shells good? Student: Because maybe something that would eat coral, coral comes up [inaudible]. Mr. W: Like, it's like a suit of armor, right? Like you bounce off of it. Like think of a turtle shell, right? If it's hard, it's harder to get through.	 • Mr. Weinberg uses his hands to show students how the cup-shaped skeleton works and explains that it is like armor or a turtle shell. • We think that it will take more grappling for students in both Ms. Hatt's and Mr. Weinberg's classrooms to put together the information about the polyp's cup-shaped skeleton, how adult polyps get their food, and the connection between the skeletons of living and dead polyps and the growth of the coral reef.

Video Episodes 4.4.1 and 4.4.2: Evidence of Student Learning

Once again, we selected two video episodes for you to watch. The first episode captures part of an after-discussion interview with Nick, a student in Ms. Hatt's class. The second is part of an interview with Darrell. As you watch these video episodes, consider what evidence they provide for student learning. Take notes about your conclusions and compare them with ours.

4.4.1: Evidence of Student Learning: Nick (1:33)

Video Episode 4.4.1: Evidence of Student Learning: Nick	Our Notes
Interviewer: So, Nick, tell me a little bit about what you learned in the discussion today. Nick: That coral is related to jellyfish, which I did not know, because if you look at coral and then look at jellyfish, they look nothing alike. Interviewer: So how are they related? Nick: Because they both have tentacles around their mouth to help them catch food. And they both are like—and their bodies are both like a water sac. Interviewer: Cool. What else did you learn? Nick: That algae w—lives in coral polyps, and the algae h—the coral helps the algae, and the algae helps the coral live. Interviewer: Oh. How, how does that happen? Nick: Wh—what happen? I got a little confused for a second. Interviewer: How does what happen? Is that what you're asking me? Oh, how does it help each other to live? Nick: Oh. The coral will live in places—the coral will l—the coral will live in places that is a lot of sunlight for the algae to g—get enough sunlight. And so the algae would get energy, and the energy in the c—the algae gives the coral nutrients and oxygen to live.	• It's interesting that Nick begins by talking about something that he "did not know": the relationship between corals and jellyfish. During the discussion, Nick had provided lots of information about jellyfish. • Here, Nick describes key aspects of the interdependence of coral polyps and algae.

4.4.2: Evidence of Student Learning: Darrell (2:00)

Video Episode 4.4.2: Evidence of Student Learning: Darrell	Our Notes
Interviewer: So, Darrell, I'm interested in finding out what you learned in your discussion today. And I know that you wrote down some things on your clipboard there. Will you share those with us? Darrell: Well, I learned that algae gives the coral nutrients and oxygen, oxygen that it needs to survive. But if it—if the algae left like in the pictures, it would soon die because the algae is not giving anything to the coral. Interviewer: So what would die if the algae left, if there was no algae? Darrell: The coral would die. Interviewer: Oh, OK. Great. What else did you learn there?	• Darrell focuses on one aspect of the coral polyp/algae interdependence right away: what the algae provide the coral. He makes reference to the illustration in the text that portrays the loss of algae and the death of coral, or coral bleaching.
Darrell: That also global warming is— Scientists believe that gl—global warming is something that makes coral die bec—is get coral stressed, because when people burn gas, fuel, and the fuel rises, the higher rises and goes to the atmosphere, and it gets trapped. And then that makes the water warmer, water warmer, and that—and the coral, it gets stressed by warmer temperatures in the water. Interviewer: Mm-hmm. Is that the only theory, that the coral gets stressed, or could something else? Darrell: The algae could also get stressed by the warmer water. Interviewer: OK. And then what was your third thing that you learned?	• Here, Darrell uses the word *stressed* and connects global warming and its effect on the stressing and eventual death of coral.
Darrell: That coral bleaching—that the coral bleaching when the coral dies—I mean, not dies, but in the stages of dying—the algae leaves, and the coral gets bleached. Yeah.	• Here, Darrell explicitly connects coral bleaching to the departure of the algae.

Discussion Moves Demonstrated in the Video Episodes

We selected the video episodes that you viewed while reading this chapter to demonstrate the discussion moves summarized below.

- Video Episode 4.1: Clear Cues
    - Be direct and clear in providing directions.
    - Be explicit about sharing with students your thinking and actions during reading: Ms. Hatt talked about her use of graphics to supplement text information.
    - Provide examples to demonstrate general concepts: Ms. Hatt provided examples of poetic language.
    - Acknowledge student contributions that provide useful insights.
- Video Episode 4.2: Providing Frameworks for Thinking About Text Information
    - Use tables as concrete frameworks to organize information that students will provide.
    - Provide verbal frameworks to organize student thinking and comments (e.g., compare/contrast, similar/different).
- Video Episodes 4.3.1 and 4.3.2: Grappling With Important Ideas
    - Recognize complex text ideas and provide enough time and support for students to grapple with them.

Take It Away

We encourage you to use the discussion plan for "Coral Reefs" with your students. We also strongly recommend that you audiotape or videotape the discussion and transcribe key episodes. Analyze the transcripts by focusing on your discussion moves and how students responded to them. Interview some students after the discussion to find out what they learned.

Use the transcript analysis tools in Appendix A to guide your analysis.

CHAPTER 5

Planning and Discussing "Jade Burial Suits"

In this chapter, we work with the text "Jade Burial Suits" by Michael Priestley. Once again, the chapter also includes video episodes of a discussion of the text. As in Chapter 4, we describe how we revised some of our thinking and planning based on experiences we had while observing teachers enacting the initial discussion plan and from our own rereading of the text.

Careful Reading of the Text

Read "Jade Burial Suits," which appears on the following pages. Write on your copy of the text and use sticky notes to capture your ideas about the content, text features, and potential opportunities for developing disciplinary knowledge that the text presents.

JADE
BURIAL SUITS

by Michael Priestley

The burial suit of Prince Liu Sheng

Princess Dou Wan's burial suit

ONE AFTERNOON IN 1968, local farm workers in Mancheng, China, were digging on a hillside. As they dug into the soil, a gaping hole suddenly appeared. One worker nearly fell into it!

When the workers climbed down into the hole, they found a set of stone doors. The doors had been sealed with molten iron and could not be opened. Soldiers were soon called in, and they blew the doors open with explosives. Inside was a tomb filled with treasures!

Bronze vase found in Prince Liu Sheng's tomb

TOMBS FOR A PRINCE AND PRINCESS

Archaeologists were called in next to explore the tomb. Based on artifacts found inside the tomb, archaeologists determined that it was the final resting place of Liu Sheng (lyoo sheng), a prince during the Han Dynasty. He died more than 2,000 years ago in about 113 BCE.

Workers soon found a second tomb nearby. It was the tomb of his wife, Princess Dou Wan (doh wahn). Archaeologists found some remarkable things in both tombs.

The tombs were large chambers dug out of the mountainside. Each tomb had an entranceway, two side rooms for storage, a large central hall, and a chamber in the back where the coffin was placed.

One of the side rooms (to the north) held jars of wine, grains, meats, and other foods. In the other side room (to the south) were chariots and the remains of horses.

The central hall was set up for a large banquet with wooden canopies and tables set for guests. Near the tables were pots, utensils, and clay figures made to look like servants.

At the back of the tomb was the burial chamber. It was lined with stone slabs. In addition to the coffin, it contained stone figures of servants, lamps, incense burners, and wine flasks. In short, the tomb held everything the prince might want in the afterlife.

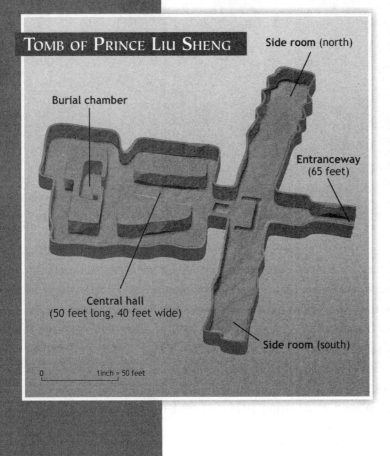

TOMB OF PRINCE LIU SHENG

Side room (north)

Burial chamber

Entranceway (65 feet)

Central hall (50 feet long, 40 feet wide)

Side room (south)

0   1inch = 50 feet

THE HAN DYNASTY

China's kingdoms began more than 3,500 years ago with the Shang dynasty. A *dynasty* is a sequence of rulers from the same family or group. Some dynasties lasted a very long time. They usually came to an end as a result of war or other major events.

By the time of the Han dynasty (206 BCE–221 CE), China was a huge empire enjoying an era of peace. It had become very wealthy through trade, especially trade with foreign countries via the Silk Road.

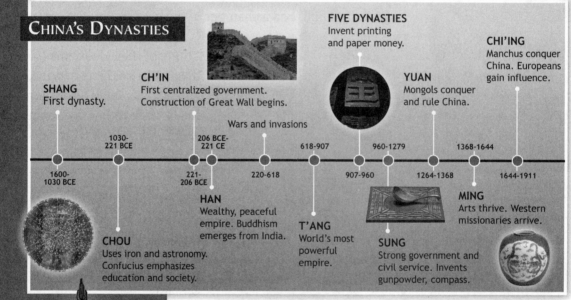

CHINA'S DYNASTIES

FIVE DYNASTIES
Invent printing and paper money.

CHI'ING
Manchus conquer China. Europeans gain influence.

SHANG
First dynasty.

CH'IN
First centralized government. Construction of Great Wall begins.

YUAN
Mongols conquer and rule China.

Wars and invasions

1030-221 BCE

206 BCE-221 CE

618-907

960-1279

1368-1644

1600-1030 BCE

221-206 BCE

220-618

907-960

1264-1368

1644-1911

HAN
Wealthy, peaceful empire. Buddhism emerges from India.

CHOU
Uses iron and astronomy. Confucius emphasizes education and society.

T'ANG
World's most powerful empire.

SUNG
Strong government and civil service. Invents gunpowder, compass.

MING
Arts thrive. Western missionaries arrive.

Also during the Han dynasty, Buddhism was emerging in China. This was a religion that began in India and spread into China and many other places. The people of China began to practice Buddhism and adopted its central belief that people have an afterlife—that a person's soul lives on after death.

Rulers in the time of the Han dynasty began planning for the afterlife. Many years before their deaths, they hired workers and slaves to dig tombs for them. In those tombs, they placed everything they thought they might need after they died.

JADE BURIAL SUITS | 3

BURIAL SUITS

When archaeologists reached the burial chamber of Liu Sheng, they made an astonishing discovery. Prince Liu Sheng had been buried in a full-body suit made of jade. Dou Wan was buried in one, too!

In ancient China, jade was thought to have special powers. It was found mainly in mountains and riverbeds, and it represented the strength of the earth. It could ward off evil spirits and protect the body from decay. Liu Sheng and his wife were buried in jade suits for protection. This would be very important if the soul remained within the body after death. However, when the suits were discovered centuries later, there was nothing left inside them but crumbled skeletons.

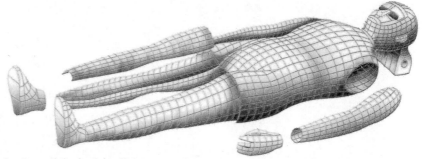

Sections of the burial suit

Each burial suit was made of 12 or more sections to cover the entire body, including the face and feet. Liu's suit was made with more than 2,500 pieces of green jade. Each piece, or plaque, was rectangular, from ½ to just under 2 inches long, and about ¹⁄₁₀ of an inch thick. Every piece of jade had holes drilled in all four corners, and the pieces were tied together with gold thread. In some burial suits, the chest piece had jade plaques glued to cloth.

Princess Dou Wan's suit was made with 2,156 pieces of jade. They were sewn together with silver thread, as befitted a princess.

WHAT IS JADE?

Jade (called "yu" in China) is a gemstone used to make jewelry and other objects. Technically, it is one of two minerals, nephrite or jadeite. Both are considered jade, but jadeite is less common and more valuable.

Jade is generally a rich green color, or greenish-white. But it may also be pink, white, red, black, brown, or violet.

Different types of jade are found mainly in Asia and Central and South America. The best deep green "imperial jade" comes from Myanmar (or Burma) in South Asia. In the ancient Mayan and Aztec civilizations of Central America, jade was considered more valuable than gold.

The word *jade* comes from a Spanish word meaning "stone of the loins." The loin refers to the pelvic area of the human body. Long ago, jade was thought to cure kidney diseases and kidney stones. (In fact, *nephrite* comes from the root word for "kidney.")

JADE BURIAL SUITS | 4

Close-up of a jade plaque tied with gold thread

During the Han dynasty, social rank was very important, and people's burial suits reflected their rank and wealth. Emperors, kings, and princes got gold thread. Dukes, princesses, and wealthy nobles got silver thread. Others got copper thread or red silk.

Only the wealthiest people could afford jade burial suits, though. Jade, gold, and silver were extremely valuable, and working with jade took great skill. An experienced craftsman would take at least ten years to cut, shape, and drill enough jade pieces for a single burial suit. One historical record suggests that more than 100 skilled craftsmen worked more than two years to construct the jade suit for Liu Sheng.

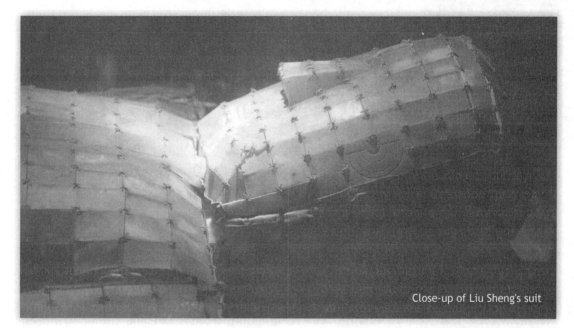
Close-up of Liu Sheng's suit

Because the jade and gold were so valuable, nobles did not want anyone breaking into their tombs to steal them. To protect their bodies and their suits, nobles built tombs with solid stone walls and sealed the doors with iron.

The custom of the jade burial suit began around 180 BCE and continued until about 222 CE. As the Han dynasty came to an end, jade burial suits were outlawed. They were considered too extravagant and too time-consuming to make.

Jade dragon

Jade burial suits were mentioned in literature and folk tales for hundreds of years, but no one was sure they actually existed until the first was discovered in 1954. Between then and 1996, a total of 18 tombs with 49 partial or complete jade burial suits were unearthed. Only 8 of those tombs contained suits made with gold thread. Most of the tombs were found in eastern China within a few hundred miles of Beijing (bay jing). Today, you can see many of these burial suits in Chinese museums.

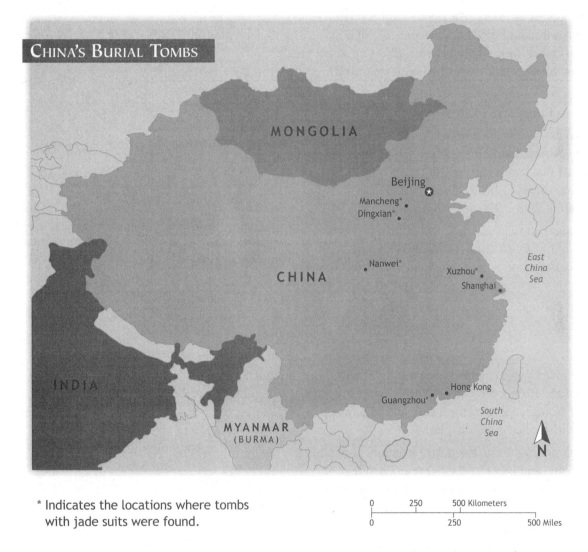

CHINA'S BURIAL TOMBS

* Indicates the locations where tombs with jade suits were found.

0   250   500 Kilometers
0   250   500 Miles

Compare your notations with ours below.

Text	Our Notes
page 1	
Jade Burial Suits by Michael Priestley One afternoon in 1968, local farm workers in Mancheng, China, were digging on a hillside. As they dug into the soil, a gaping hole suddenly appeared. One worker nearly fell into it! When the workers climbed down into the hole, they found a set of stone doors. The doors had been sealed with molten iron and could not be opened. Soldiers were soon called in, and they blew the doors open with explosives. Inside was a tomb filled with treasures!	• This section provides an interesting opening to the text and raises the question, What were the treasures? • Showing China on a world map will provide an important reference point for students. • The photographs on this page are not to the same scale. The photo of Dou Wan's burial suit looks like it's for a doll rather than a person.
page 2	
Tombs for a Prince and Princess Archaeologists were called in next to explore the tomb. Based on artifacts found inside the tomb, archaeologists determined that it was the final resting place of Liu Sheng (lyoo sheng), a prince during the Han Dynasty. He died more than 2,000 years ago in about 113 BCE. Workers soon found a second tomb nearby. It was the tomb of his wife, Princess Dou Wan (doh wahn). Archaeologists found some remarkable things in both tombs.	• *Artifact* is a key term in the text. An artifact is something crafted or made by humans. The bronze vase in the photograph is an artifact. • Students will need an explanation of *BCE*, which stands for "Before the Common Era." The year 113 BCE refers to 113 years before what is commonly referred to as the year 1. • The prince died 113 years before the year 1 and his body was discovered in 1968, so that's 113 + 1,968, or 2,081 years before the discovery. • How would the artifacts help archaeologists figure out that it was the tomb of Liu Sheng?
The tombs were large chambers dug out of the mountainside. Each tomb had an entranceway, two side rooms for storage, a large central hall, and a chamber in the back where the coffin was placed. One of the side rooms (to the north) held jars of wine, grains, meats, and other foods. In the other side room (to the south) were chariots and the remains of horses. The central hall was set up for a large banquet with wooden canopies and tables set for guests. Near the tables were pots, utensils, and clay figures made to look like servants. At the back of the tomb was the burial chamber. It was lined with stone slabs. In addition to the coffin, it contained stone figures of servants, lamps, incense burners, and wine flasks. In short, the tomb held everything the prince might want in the afterlife.	• Students can use the diagram on this page and a ruler to figure out just how large the tombs were. • The diagram connects directly to the text, showing the layout of the tomb. • All the artifacts and other items in the tomb tell a story about the life and beliefs of the prince and princess, but that story isn't obvious. The artifacts are clues that need to be interpreted. • This information about the tomb will probably remind students of Egyptian tombs.

(continued)

Text	Our Notes
The Han Dynasty China's kingdoms began more than 3,500 years ago with the Shang dynasty. A *dynasty* is a sequence of rulers from the same family or group. Some dynasties lasted a very long time. They usually came to an end as a result of war or other major events.	• This section of the text functions as an interlude. Readers are stepping out of the narrative about the archaeological discovery of the tombs to learn about the Han dynasty.
By the time of the Han dynasty (206 BCE–221 CE), China was a huge empire enjoying an era of peace. It had become very wealthy through trade, especially trade with foreign countries via the Silk Road.	• The Silk Road (show on world map) was a network of trade routes across land and sea, linking Asia, Europe, and Africa. The Silk Road got its name from the Chinese silk trade, which began during the Han dynasty. It extended for 4,000 miles (6,500 km). • Traders brought not only products but also ideas. The Silk Road was also an important route for the spread of the Black Death in the Middle Ages.
China's Dynasties (timeline)	• This shows the beginning of the Han dynasty in 206 BCE, its demise in 221 CE, and the long period of wars and invasions from 220 to 618 CE before the emergence of the T'ang dynasty in 618 CE. • This also includes information that helps a reader understand why the context—in terms of religion, prosperity, and peace in the region—was conducive to the making of jade suits and huge tombs.
Also during the Han dynasty, Buddhism was emerging in China. This was a religion that began in India and spread into China and many other places. The people of China began to practice Buddhism and adopted its central belief that people have an afterlife—that a person's soul lives on after death.	• One of Buddhism's central beliefs is rebirth. A person's spirit is reborn after death into many possible forms: a higher form (e.g., a spiritual being), a lower form (e.g., an animal), or the same human form. • The Chinese belief in an afterlife as described here seems to represent the afterlife as a rebirth into the human form because the artifacts in the tomb are things that humans would need.
Rulers in the time of the Han dynasty began planning for the afterlife. Many years before their deaths, they hired workers and slaves to dig tombs for them. In those tombs, they placed everything they thought they might need after they died.	*(continued)*

Text	Our Notes
page 4	
Burial Suits	• This section picks up the narrative of the archaeological discovery.
When archaeologists reached the burial chamber of Liu Sheng, they made an astonishing discovery. Prince Liu Sheng had been buried in a full-body suit made of jade. Dou Wan was buried in one, too!	
In ancient China, jade was thought to have special powers. It was found mainly in mountains and riverbeds, and it represented the strength of the earth. It could ward off evil spirits and protect the body from decay. Liu Sheng and his wife were buried in jade suits for protection. This would be very important if the soul remained within the body after death. However, when the suits were discovered centuries later, there was nothing left inside them but crumbled skeletons.	• Jade was chosen to create the suits because people believed it had special powers. One power was to protect the body from decay. • The Chinese beliefs about the afterlife are complex. The information here adds to the previous information about the Chinese belief in the afterlife. It seems that they believed that the spirit would come into the same body it had.
Each burial suit was made of 12 or more sections to cover the entire body, including the face and feet. Liu's suit was made with more than 2,500 pieces of green jade. Each piece, or plaque, was rectangular, from ½ to just under 2 inches long, and about ¹⁄₁₀ of an inch thick. Every piece of jade had holes drilled in all four corners, and the pieces were tied together with gold thread. In some burial suits, the chest piece had jade plaques glued to cloth. Princess Dou Wan's suit was made with 2,156 pieces of jade. They were sewn together with silver thread, as befitted a princess.	• The photographs on pages 1 and 5 show the jade tiles. • The important idea here is that the jade burial suits were extremely complicated to make.
page 4 sidebar	
What Is Jade?	• The information in this sidebar is interesting but can distract attention from the text.
Jade (called "yu" in China) is a gemstone used to make jewelry and other objects. Technically, it is one of two minerals, nephrite or jadeite. Both are considered jade, but jadeite is less common and more valuable.	• It's not important for understanding the text, so it could be read later, or students could read it on their own.
Jade is generally a rich green color, or greenish-white. But it may also be pink, white, red, black, brown, or violet.	
Different types of jade are found mainly in Asia and Central and South America. The best deep green "imperial jade" comes from Myanmar (or Burma) in South Asia. In the ancient Mayan and Aztec civilizations of Central America, jade was considered more valuable than gold.	
The word *jade* comes from a Spanish word meaning "stone of the loins." The loin refers to the pelvic area of the human body. Long ago, jade was thought to cure kidney diseases and kidney stones. (In fact, *nephrite* comes from the root word for "kidney.")	*(continued)*

Text	Our Notes
page 5	
During the Han dynasty, social rank was very important, and people's burial suits reflected their rank and wealth. Emperors, kings, and princes got gold thread. Dukes, princesses, and wealthy nobles got silver thread. Others got copper thread or red silk.	• More details are given about the creation of the jade suits, but this time the information relates to the social ranks in Chinese society.
Only the wealthiest people could afford jade burial suits, though. Jade, gold, and silver were extremely valuable, and working with jade took great skill. An experienced craftsman would take at least ten years to cut, shape, and drill enough jade pieces for a single burial suit. One historical record suggests that more than 100 skilled craftsmen worked more than two years to construct the jade suit for Liu Sheng.	• All the careful work and time it took to make the jade suits indicate that royalty must have had strong beliefs about their power and importance. • The historical record mentioned here might be a log that craftsmen filled out on the days they worked. Perhaps the log was used to calculate the payments owed to the craftsmen.
Because the jade and gold were so valuable, nobles did not want anyone breaking into their tombs to steal them. To protect their bodies and their suits, nobles built tombs with solid stone walls and sealed the doors with iron.	• The information about the stone walls and sealing the doors with iron connects to the information on page 1.
The custom of the jade burial suit began around 180 BCE and continued until about 222 CE. As the Han dynasty came to an end, jade burial suits were outlawed. They were considered too extravagant and too time-consuming to make.	• The outlawing of the jade suits makes sense given the information on the timeline about the wars and invasions at the time. • The outlawing also reveals something about changes in the beliefs of Chinese royalty.
page 6	
Jade burial suits were mentioned in literature and folk tales for hundreds of years, but no one was sure they actually existed until the first was discovered in 1954. Between then and 1996, a total of 18 tombs with 49 partial or complete jade burial suits were unearthed. Only 8 of those tombs contained suits made with gold thread. Most of the tombs were found in eastern China within a few hundred miles of Beijing (bay jing). Today, you can see many of these burial suits in Chinese museums.	• The idea of the jade suits being mentioned in literature and folk tales is interesting. It makes sense that a complicated and expensive suit with power to preserve the human body from decay would be featured in stories.

Analyzing "Jade Burial Suits"

Content

"Jade Burial Suits" provides a detailed account of extraordinary artifacts—jade burial suits—that reveal much about a specific time in Chinese history: the Han dynasty. The jade burial suits provide information about the ranks in Han society, the availability of wealth and time to create the suits, and the importance of beliefs in an afterlife.

Focusing students' attention on the jade burial suits as artifacts that reveal information about a specific historical period allows students to organize the text information into a coherent mental representation, or situation model, rather than just a collection of interesting facts.

The text does not provide a full explanation of beliefs about the afterlife and how they relate to the purpose of the jade suits and the objects that were placed in the tomb. If the jade suits were meant to preserve the bodies of the dead, students may wonder if the prince and princess were supposed to come back to life and return to their former lives. If so, how would they get out of the tombs with their heavy stone doors that were sealed tightly with molten iron?

Students may also wonder about the items in the tombs. Real chariots, horses, food, and wine were included, but only clay and stone figures of servants were found.

Research

We conducted research related to the following topics to prepare for designing the discussion plan for "Jade Burial Suits."

- *Archaeology:* Archaeology is considered to be both a scientific field and a subject in the humanities. In the United States, it is considered a branch of anthropology. There are many subfields in archaeology, but the main purpose of the field is to provide information about how people lived in the past.

- *Buddhism:* Buddhism is considered to be a religion as well as a philosophy. It encompasses a complex set of traditions, beliefs, and practices. The notion of rebirth is a central tenet of Buddhism. Beings are reborn over and over again until they reach the blissful state of nirvana. Rebirth into higher or lower forms is based on the helpful or hurtful decisions that people make during their lives and the consequences of those decisions.

- *Pyramids of ancient Egypt:* Students may connect the Chinese tombs to the pyramid tombs of ancient Egypt. The famous Egyptian pyramids at Giza were built in 2589 BCE. At the present time, 138 pyramids have been excavated in Egypt. The tombs described in "Jade Burial Suits" were built in 113 BCE, more than 2,400 years later than the Egyptian pyramids. To date, only 18 tombs with jade burial suits have been found in China.

Text Features

The text provides opportunities for focusing on important headings, photographs, diagrams, and timeline.

- *Headings:* The headings provide a way to organize the information in the text into sections.

- *Photographs:* The text is illustrated with dramatic photographs of jade burial suits, including close-ups, as well as other artifacts.

- *Diagram:* The diagram of Prince Liu Sheng's tomb on page 2 includes a scale that can be used to calculate its size. The diagram provides a spatial representation of information in the text.
- *Timeline:* The timeline on page 3 provides important information about the Han and other dynasties. The timeline supplies information needed to understand why the Han dynasty declined.

Disciplinary Knowledge

"Jade Burial Suits" provides an opportunity for students to learn about the importance of the work done by historical archaeologists. Historical archaeologists investigate artifacts and other physical evidence, such as structures created by people from the past, to understand how people lived and what they believed. Historical archaeologists excavate buildings, homes, and tombs and the objects they contain to reconstruct the past.

Selecting Learning Goals

We think it will be useful for you to see how our thinking developed from the initial discussion plan to subsequent versions. In the table below, we show our initial set of learning goals and the set that we developed after watching the lesson plan enacted in classrooms and analyzing the text in a more rigorous way. Compare our first set of goals (take 1) with our second set (take 2).

Take 1	Take 2
How did ancient Chinese people's beliefs in the afterlife—shaped by Buddhism—influence their practices in burying the dead?	**What story do the jade burial suits and the tombs in which they were found tell about the society, economy, politics, and beliefs of the Han dynasty?**
• An important Buddhist belief is that a person who dies is either reborn into another body or form, or enters nirvana (a state of perfect bliss and peace). Most people are reborn because they do not attain enlightenment, and therefore are not yet worthy to attain nirvana.	• The jade burial suits and the tombs in which they were found reveal that their society was organized into ranks, including emperors, kings, princes, dukes, princesses, and nobles. A large class of craftsmen to create the jade suits and workers to build the tombs must have existed as well.
• The idea of the dead returning to life influenced the burial practices of the ancient Chinese—at least the burial practices for royalty. Princes and princesses had elaborate tombs with everything they might need. Many were also buried in suits of jade, which were supposed to protect the body from decay and evil spirits.	• Members of the royalty believed in an afterlife and were buried in jade suits that were supposed to preserve their bodies and ward off evil spirits. Objects buried in tombs offer more evidence of a belief in an afterlife.
How do people today learn about the ancient past?	• During the Han dynasty, there was enough wealth to create jade suits and to construct large tombs.
• Artifacts, historical records, literature, and folklore provide archaeologists with important information and interpretations of life in ancient times.	• There was also peace, so the wealth could be used for the tombs and suits instead of for weapons, and workers and craftsmen could create the suits and build the tombs instead of fighting enemies.

We see our initial learning goals (take 1) as being focused on important text information but without explicit reference to how those ideas might be organized into a coherent mental representation, or situation model. The second set of goals (take 2) makes the important organizing idea of the society, economy, politics, and beliefs of the Han dynasty much more obvious.

Take 1	Take 2 (These goals did not change.)
How can graphics support readers in understanding the text more deeply?	**How can graphics support readers in understanding the text more deeply?**
• Photographs, including close-ups, allow readers to see the jade suits in detail.	• Photographs, including close-ups, allow readers to see the jade suits in detail.
• A diagram provides information about the interior of the prince's tomb.	• A diagram provides information about the interior of the prince's tomb.
• The timeline provides a way for readers to see the chronological context of events described in the text.	• The timeline provides a way for readers to see the chronological context of events described in the text.
• The illustration provides more information about how the jade suits were made.	• The illustration provides more information about how the jade suits were made.
• The map shows the places where tombs with jade suits have been found.	• The map shows the places where tombs with jade suits have been found.

Designing the Exit

We created several versions of an exit for a discussion of "Jade Burial Suits." We kept in mind the learning goals, but also the need to keep the activity short enough to complete after the discussion. As you can see by reading the versions below, the language in our exit became more precise and focused on the most important aspects of the situation model in the text.

- *Take 1:* Arrange students into groups of four and pose the following challenge: You're on an archaeological team that has uncovered a tomb, complete with a jade suit. Journalists found out about it and come rushing to the site. They ask you two questions:
  - What did you find in there?
  - What does it mean?

  Work with your group to be ready to answer these questions.
- *Take 2:* What do the jade suits tell us about the Han dynasty—how people lived and what they believed?
- *Take 3:* If Prince Liu Sheng and Princess Dou Wan could speak to us, what might they say about what their lives were like and why they were buried in jade suits?
- *Take 4:* Complete the following sentences:
  - I am Princess Dou Wan, and I...
  - I lived in China in the Han dynasty, a time when...
  - I was buried in a jade suit because...

We think the final version comes closest to eliciting a situation model from students.

Designing the Launch

We had several ideas about how to launch a discussion of "Jade Burial Suits."

Take 1

In the initial plan, we suggested that teachers display a map of China and explain that students would be reading about discoveries in China that took place in 1968. We also suggested that students read the title, look at the photographs, and talk about what they notice.

Take 2

To give students a sense of the discovery of the tombs and how archaeologists analyzed the artifacts they found there, we thought about asking students to think about people from the future examining a landfill and trying to figure out how we live now from what they discover.

Take 3

After considering Take 2, we thought that it was too general. We decided to engage students in visualizing a scenario that would more closely resemble the discovery of the sealed tombs. Here's the guided visualization that we created:

Imagine that there's a huge flood. In fact, it's so huge that it buries our school under many feet of mud. Years go by, and the mud hardens. Trees grow there, and it looks like a hill.

One day, people decide to build in the area. They begin to dig to lay the foundations of new homes. Imagine their amazement when they find what turns out to be the roof of a building! They push through the roof and lower themselves into what was once our classroom.

Imagine these people looking in your desk, through the bookshelves, and at the computer stations. Imagine them walking through the building into the cafeteria, the media center, the kindergarten classroom, and the main hallway where the glass trophy cases are.

What would these objects and rooms tell about how we live now and what we think is important?

Today we're going to read an informational article about an event very similar to this, but it takes place in China.

We see this launch as introducing students to the situation model captured in the learning goal: how artifacts reveal information about the society, economy, politics, and beliefs of people from the past.

Designing the Discussion Plan

In the section that follows, we show how our analysis of the text and the learning goals that we selected informed a discussion plan for "Jade Burial Suits." We offer the plan not as a script but as an example of a discussion about the text that could be enacted to support student comprehension.

Discussion Plan for "Jade Burial Suits"

Learning Goals

1. What story do the jade burial suits and the tombs in which they were found tell about the society, economy, politics, and beliefs of the Han dynasty?

   - The jade burial suits and the tombs in which they were found reveal that their society was organized into ranks, including emperors, kings, princes, dukes, princesses, and nobles. A large class of craftsmen to create the jade suits and workers to build the tombs must have existed as well.

   - Members of the royalty believed in an afterlife and were buried in jade suits that were supposed to preserve their bodies and ward off evil spirits. Objects buried in tombs offer more evidence of a belief in an afterlife.

   - During the Han dynasty, there was enough wealth to create jade suits and to construct large tombs.

   - There was also peace, so the wealth could be used for the tombs and suits instead of for weapons, and workers and craftsmen could create the suits and build the tombs instead of fighting enemies.

2. How can graphics support readers in understanding the text more deeply?

   - Photographs, including close-ups, allow readers to see the jade suits in detail.

   - A diagram provides information about the interior of the prince's tomb.

   - The timeline provides a way for readers to see the chronological context of events described in the text.

   - The illustration provides more information about how the jade suits were made.

   - The map shows the places where tombs with jade suits have been found.

Resources

- Copies of "Jade Burial Suits"
- World map
- Rulers
- Samples of jade (optional)
- Task sheets with the following task:

  Complete the following sentences:
  - I am Princess Dou Wan, and I...
  - I lived in China in the Han dynasty, a time when...
  - I was buried in a jade suit because...

As part of your preparation, measure the length and width of your classroom.

Launch

Distribute copies of "Jade Burial Suits." Indicate the location of China on a world map.

Imagine that there's a huge flood. In fact, it's so huge that it buries our school under many feet of mud. Years go by, and the mud hardens. Trees grow there, and it looks like a hill.

One day, people decide to build in the area. They begin to dig to lay the foundations of new homes. Imagine their amazement when they find what turns out to be the roof of a building! They push through the roof and lower themselves into what was once our classroom.

Imagine these people looking in your desk, through the bookshelves, and at the computer stations. Imagine them walking through the building into the cafeteria, the media center, the kindergarten classroom, and the main hallway where the glass trophy cases are.

What would these objects and rooms tell about how we live now and what we think is important?

Today we're going to read an informational article about an event very similar to this, but it takes place in China.

The **bolded** text in the table below provides instructions for what you should do. Instructions to read, for example, mean that you or a volunteer should read the indicated text aloud.

Text	Our Notes	Reader–Text Interactions
page 1		
Jade Burial Suits by Michael Priestley One afternoon in 1968, local farm workers in Mancheng, China, were digging on a hillside. As they dug into the soil, a gaping hole suddenly appeared. One worker nearly fell into it! When the workers climbed down into the hole, they found a set of stone doors. The doors had been sealed with molten iron and could not be opened. Soldiers were soon called in, and they blew the doors open with explosives. Inside was a tomb filled with treasures!	• This section provides an interesting opening to the text and raises the question, What were the treasures? • Showing China on a world map will provide an important reference point for students. • The photographs on this page are not to the same scale. The photo of Dou Wan's burial suit looks like it's for a doll rather than a person.	• **Read the title, author's name, and captions on this page.** • **Locate China on a world map.** • **Ask students to talk about the photos and what they notice.** • *What is a burial suit?* • **Some students may think that the princess is standing, so remind them that she is enclosed in a burial suit.** • **Read the two paragraphs on this page.** • *What have we found out so far?* • **Check to be sure that students understand what a tomb is.** *(continued)*

Text	Our Notes	Reader–Text Interactions
page 2		

Text	Our Notes	Reader–Text Interactions
Tombs for a Prince and Princess Archaeologists were called in next to explore the tomb. Based on artifacts found inside the tomb, archaeologists determined that it was the final resting place of Liu Sheng (lyoo sheng), a prince during the Han Dynasty. He died more than 2,000 years ago in about 113 BCE. Workers soon found a second tomb nearby. It was the tomb of his wife, Princess Dou Wan (doh wahn). Archaeologists found some remarkable things in both tombs.	• *Artifact* is a key term in the text. An artifact is something crafted or made by humans. The bronze vase in the photograph is an artifact. • Students will need an explanation of *BCE*, which stands for "Before the Common Era." The year 113 BCE refers to 113 years before what is commonly referred to as the year 1. • The prince died 113 years before the year 1 and his body was discovered in 1968, so that's 113 + 1,968, or 2,081 years before the discovery. • How would the artifacts help archaeologists figure out that it was the tomb of Liu Sheng?	• **Read the first two paragraphs.** • *Another word for* treasures *is* artifacts. *The bronze vase in the photograph is an artifact.* • BCE *stands for "Before the Common Era," or 113 years before what is commonly referred to as year 1. The prince died 113 years before the year 1, and his body was discovered in 1968, so that's 113 + 1968, or 2,081 years before the discovery.* • *Remember, it was the soldiers who first came across this set of sealed doors. They must have been very curious to know what was behind them. Why do you think they stopped and called in the archaeologists? What do archaeologists do?*
The tombs were large chambers dug out of the mountainside. Each tomb had an entranceway, two side rooms for storage, a large central hall, and a chamber in the back where the coffin was placed. One of the side rooms (to the north) held jars of wine, grains, meats, and other foods. In the other side room (to the south) were chariots and the remains of horses. The central hall was set up for a large banquet with wooden canopies and tables set for guests. Near the tables were pots, utensils, and clay figures made to look like servants. At the back of the tomb was the burial chamber. It was lined with stone slabs. In addition to the coffin, it contained stone figures of servants, lamps, incense burners, and wine flasks. In short, the tomb held everything the prince might want in the afterlife.	• Students can use the diagram on this page and a ruler to figure out just how large the tombs were. • The diagram connects directly to the text, showing the layout of the tomb. • All the artifacts and other items in the tomb tell a story about the life and beliefs of the prince and princess, but that story isn't obvious. The artifacts are clues that need to be interpreted. • This information about the tomb will probably remind students of Egyptian tombs.	• **Read the rest of the page.** • **Use the scale bar on the diagram and a ruler to calculate the size of the tomb.** • *How long was the tomb?* • *How wide was it?* • **Compare the tomb's dimensions with your classroom's.** • *How many classrooms like ours would fit inside the tomb?* • *The last sentence seems to suggest that in the afterlife, the prince will be like he was when he was alive. So far, we don't have enough information to understand what the Chinese believed about the afterlife.*

(continued)

Text	Our Notes	Reader–Text Interactions
page 3		
The Han Dynasty China's kingdoms began more than 3,500 years ago with the Shang dynasty. A *dynasty* is a sequence of rulers from the same family or group. Some dynasties lasted a very long time. They usually came to an end as a result of war or other major events. By the time of the Han dynasty (206 BCE–221 CE), China was a huge empire enjoying an era of peace. It had become very wealthy through trade, especially trade with foreign countries via the Silk Road.	• This section of the text functions as an interlude. Readers are stepping out of the narrative about the archaeological discovery of the tombs to learn about the Han dynasty. • The Silk Road (show on world map) was a network of trade routes across land and sea, linking Asia, Europe, and Africa. The Silk Road got its name from the Chinese silk trade, which began during the Han dynasty. It extended for 4,000 miles (6,500 km). • Traders brought not only products but also ideas. The Silk Road was also an important route for the spread of the Black Death in the Middle Ages.	• *We've been learning about the tombs, but now we're stopping to find out about the time in which the tombs were built.* • **Read the first two paragraphs.** • **Explain what the Silk Road was and trace its route on a world map.**
China's Dynasties (timeline)	• This shows the beginning of the Han dynasty in 206 BCE, its demise in 221 CE, and the long period of wars and invasions from 220 to 618 CE before the emergence of the T'ang dynasty in 618 CE. • This also includes information that helps a reader understand why the context—in terms of religion, prosperity, and peace in the region—was conducive to the making of jade suits and huge tombs.	• *Like the diagram on page 2, this timeline provides information to help us understand what the text says.* • *Find the Han dynasty on the timeline.* • *What does the timeline reveal about the kind of government that existed during the Han dynasty?* • *What does the timeline reveal about why the Han dynasty ended?* *(continued)*

Text	Our Notes	Reader–Text Interactions
page 3 continued			

Text	Our Notes	Reader–Text Interactions
Also during the Han dynasty, Buddhism was emerging in China. This was a religion that began in India and spread into China and many other places. The people of China began to practice Buddhism and adopted its central belief that people have an afterlife—that a person's soul lives on after death. Rulers in the time of the Han dynasty began planning for the afterlife. Many years before their deaths, they hired workers and slaves to dig tombs for them. In those tombs, they placed everything they thought they might need after they died.	• One of Buddhism's central beliefs is rebirth. A person's spirit is reborn after death into many possible forms: a higher form (e.g., a spiritual being), a lower form (e.g., an animal), or the same human form. • The Chinese belief in an afterlife as described here seems to represent the afterlife as a rebirth into the human form because the artifacts in the tomb are things that humans would need.	• **Read the next two paragraphs.** • *Here we find out more about the afterlife.* • **Share information about Buddhism and the afterlife.** • *Again, we read about the tombs having "everything they thought they might need after they died."* • *It seems that the Chinese might believe that after death a person is reborn as a human again.*
page 4			
Burial Suits When archaeologists reached the burial chamber of Liu Sheng, they made an astonishing discovery. Prince Liu Sheng had been buried in a full-body suit made of jade. Dou Wan was buried in one, too! In ancient China, jade was thought to have special powers. It was found mainly in mountains and riverbeds, and it represented the strength of the earth. It could ward off evil spirits and protect the body from decay. Liu Sheng and his wife were buried in jade suits for protection. This would be very important if the soul remained within the body after death. However, when the suits were discovered centuries later, there was nothing left inside them but crumbled skeletons.	• This section picks up the narrative of the archaeological discovery. • Jade was chosen to create the suits because people believed it had special powers. One power was to protect the body from decay. • The Chinese beliefs about the afterlife are complex. The information here adds to the previous information about the Chinese belief in the afterlife. It seems that they believed that the spirit would come into the same body it had.	• **Read the first two paragraphs.** • *Why were the burial suits made out of jade? Why was that material chosen instead of something else?* • *What does that tell us about Chinese beliefs about the afterlife?* • *(Again, if the body was preserved, it seems to suggest that it would come back to life.)* *(continued)*

Text	Our Notes	Reader–Text Interactions
<div align="center">**page 4** *continued*</div>		
Each burial suit was made of 12 or more sections to cover the entire body, including the face and feet. Liu's suit was made with more than 2,500 pieces of green jade. Each piece, or plaque, was rectangular, from ½ to just under 2 inches long, and about 1/10 of an inch thick. Every piece of jade had holes drilled in all four corners, and the pieces were tied together with gold thread. In some burial suits, the chest piece had jade plaques glued to cloth. Princess Dou Wan's suit was made with 2,156 pieces of jade. They were sewn together with silver thread, as befitted a princess.	• The photographs on pages 1 and 5 show the jade tiles. • The important idea here is that the jade burial suits were extremely complicated to make.	• **If you have some jade, show it to students.** • **Ask students to read the captions for the photographs on page 5. Have them study these photographs and describe what they see.**
<div align="center">**page 4 sidebar**</div>		
What Is Jade? Jade (called "yu" in China) is a gemstone used to make jewelry and other objects. Technically, it is one of two minerals, nephrite or jadeite. Both are considered jade, but jadeite is less common and more valuable. Jade is generally a rich green color, or greenish-white. But it may also be pink, white, red, black, brown, or violet. Different types of jade are found mainly in Asia and Central and South America. The best deep green "imperial jade" comes from Myanmar (or Burma) in South Asia. In the ancient Mayan and Aztec civilizations of Central America, jade was considered more valuable than gold. The word *jade* comes from a Spanish word meaning "stone of the loins." The loin refers to the pelvic area of the human body. Long ago, jade was thought to cure kidney diseases and kidney stones. (In fact, *nephrite* comes from the root word for "kidney.")	• The information in this sidebar is interesting but can distract attention from the text. • It's not important for understanding the text, so it could be read later, or students could read it on their own.	• *You can read the sidebar later to learn more about jade.* • *For now, let's turn to page 5.* *(continued)*

Text	Our Notes	Reader–Text Interactions
page 5		
During the Han dynasty, social rank was very important, and people's burial suits reflected their rank and wealth. Emperors, kings, and princes got gold thread. Dukes, princesses, and wealthy nobles got silver thread. Others got copper thread or red silk.	• More details are given about the creation of the jade suits, but this time the information relates to the social ranks in Chinese society.	• **Read the first two paragraphs.** • *Archaeologists figured out what the different kinds of thread meant. The thread was a clue about society in the Han dynasty.* • *What does the first sentence mean?*
Only the wealthiest people could afford jade burial suits, though. Jade, gold, and silver were extremely valuable, and working with jade took great skill. An experienced craftsman would take at least ten years to cut, shape, and drill enough jade pieces for a single burial suit. One historical record suggests that more than 100 skilled craftsmen worked more than two years to construct the jade suit for Liu Sheng.	• All the careful work and time it took to make the jade suits indicate that royalty must have had strong beliefs about their power and importance. • The historical record mentioned here might be a log that craftsmen filled out on the days they worked. Perhaps the log was used to calculate the payments owed to the craftsmen.	
Because the jade and gold were so valuable, nobles did not want anyone breaking into their tombs to steal them. To protect their bodies and their suits, nobles built tombs with solid stone walls and sealed the doors with iron. The custom of the jade burial suit began around 180 BCE and continued until about 222 CE. As the Han dynasty came to an end, jade burial suits were outlawed. They were considered too extravagant and too time-consuming to make.	• The information about the stone walls and sealing the doors with iron connects to the information on page 1. • The outlawing of the jade suits makes sense given the information on the timeline about the wars and invasions at the time. • The outlawing also reveals something about changes in the beliefs of Chinese royalty.	• **Read the next two paragraphs.** • *Remember that at the beginning of this article, we read about the farmers finding these doors.* • *What does the decision to stop making jade suits tell us about how events were influencing religious beliefs in ancient China?* • *What was happening when the Han dynasty came to an end?* *(continued)*

Text	Our Notes	Reader–Text Interactions
page 6		
Jade burial suits were mentioned in literature and folk tales for hundreds of years, but no one was sure they actually existed until the first was discovered in 1954. Between then and 1996, a total of 18 tombs with 49 partial or complete jade burial suits were unearthed. Only 8 of those tombs contained suits made with gold thread. Most of the tombs were found in eastern China within a few hundred miles of Beijing (bay jing). Today, you can see many of these burial suits in Chinese museums.	• The idea of the jade suits being mentioned in literature and folk tales is interesting. It makes sense that a complicated and expensive suit with power to preserve the human body from decay would be featured in stories.	• **Read the paragraph.** • *Here we find out that the burial suits have been included in stories for a long time, but people thought burial suits were simply a fantastic story. Why might they not have believed in the jade suits?* • *Let's talk about the Han dynasty. What did you find out about that period of history? What was it like to live during that time? Focus on the politics, or government; the society; and the religion.*

Exit

Distribute the following task:

Complete the following sentences:

- I am Princess Dou Wan, and I…
- I lived in China in the Han dynasty, a time when…
- I was buried in a jade suit because…

Some Important Moves in the Discussion Plan

Some important moves to notice in the discussion plan for "Jade Burial Suits" include the following:

- *Providing an initial framework for thinking about the text:* The scenario of the mud-covered school provides students with a framework for thinking about the archaeologists and their investigation of the buried tombs.
- *Making it real:* Engaging students in measuring the dimensions of Liu Sheng's tomb and comparing those dimensions with the classroom's is an activity that makes text information become concrete.

Viewing Video Episodes

The video episodes for this chapter feature Ms. Hatt and her fourth-grade students.

Video Episode 5.1: Collaborating to Build an Explanation

As you watch this video episode, notice how Ms. Hatt orchestrates a collaborative effort in explaining the work of archaeologists. Take notes about what you observe and then compare them with our notes in the table below.

🔘 **5.1: Collaborating to Build an Explanation (3:48)**

Video Episode 5.1: Collaborating to Build an Explanation	Our Notes
Ms. H: The next section is called "Tombs for a Prince and Princess." [reading] "Archaeologists were called in next to explore the tomb." Hmm. Why do you think they stopped and called archaeologists? Sydney? Sydney: They could discover if it's valuable or not. Ms. H: OK. Lynn? Lynn: Archaeologists often know what to do if something happens. Th—they're trained to know what—if there's a [inaudible], they know exactly what to do to get out if there is suddenly like flooding or something and it traps them in t—in the tomb, 'cause most—a lot of archaeologists are trained to be able to survive those attacks. Ms. H: Those unexpected situations? What else do you think archaeologists know to do? Shawn? Shawn: I know a lot about archaeologists, too, and they—they're known for finding stuff and knowing like what it is or how old it is. Student: What it dates back to. Shawn: Or—yeah, like what it dates back to and— Ms. H: Say more about that. Student: Like if a archaeologist saw a vase like this, it was in the tomb, and they would look at the details in it like the small crevices and stuff like that, and that would tell them if it was something modern meant to look like it was something— Ms. H: Ancient. Student: Yeah, or something really from Egypt. Ms. H: Hmm. OK, so also— I'm sorry, Mary. I didn't see your hand go up.	• Ms. Hatt asks students to think about why the soldiers stopped and called in archaeologists. Sydney offers that the archaeologists would know if the contents of the tomb are valuable. • Lynn brings in the idea that archaeologists have special training. She also seems to refer to archaeologists who work in areas where there are natural disasters as well as dangerous places where they may be attacked during their work. • Ms. Hatt asks Lynn if she is talking about "unexpected situations," and Lynn agrees. • Ms. Hatt rephrases her question, now focusing not just on what archaeologists *do* but on what they *know*: • Another student picks up on Shawn's reference to "how old it is, " and Shawn agrees, adding more to the explanation of what archaeologists know and do.

(continued)

Video Episode 5.1: Collaborating to Build an Explanation *continued*	Our Notes
Mary: Yeah, like when ar—archaeologists like may—like maybe they go in there because then archaeologists, they—they'd know how to study— Like there's some—like sometimes they might have made something trap, like they— Like in a way I agree with Lynn, but in some ways I don't because I s—because I agree with Lynn that like the attacks, but I just don't really know. But I sort of in a way don't because if—if there was something like a flood or something, I mean, they'd probably know how to get out. But if they found some— But I think archaeologists probably pretty much only— The thing they're really known for is like not really for doing that. I think it's really, actually it's for—like they're really for try—like trying to find things, 'cause if we—any one of us try to go outside and try to dig for a treasure chest or something, we probably wouldn't find it 'cause we don't know what to like look— Like they'd probably have a map or something where like some, some schema about like different landmarks that could show there was.	• Mary refers to Lynn's earlier comment and picks up on the word *attacks*. Mary is working out her thinking here, and Ms. Hatt gives her time to do that.
Ms. H: OK. Lynn, when you say *attacks*, you mean difficult situations, right?	• Ms. Hatt listens to Mary's long comment and connects it to Lynn's idea that sometimes archaeologists work in difficult situations.
Lynn: Yeah.	
Ms. H: OK. And I'm gonna build on what all of you are saying. I think I hear you saying that they know what to look for. And I want to add on that they probably know how to handle whatever they find. So, if I was trying to dig something out or to remove something, I might hold it in a way or try to remove it in a way that could break it.	• Sometimes students offer comments that seem to be rambling, but they are working out their ideas. • Here, Ms. Hatt shares her own thinking about what archaeologists know and do—incorporating a student's contribution (fragile) as well.
Student: Or it could drop.	
Ms. H: Right? And so I think that they have tools, and they have experience handling really—	
Student: Fragile things.	
Ms. H: —fragile things.	

Video Episode 5.2: *Making the Most of a Key Graphic*

As you watch this video episode, notice how Ms. Hatt directs students to make use of the important information on the timeline. Jot down your observations and then compare yours with ours.

5.2: Making the Most of a Key Graphic (3:58)

Video Episode 5.2: Making the Most of a Key Graphic	Our Notes
Ms. H: Let's turn the page. We're on page 3, and there's a heading here: [reading] "The Han Dynasty." Let's look at the timeline before we begin and let's see if we can get some information about the Han dynasty. Remember, timelines are text features that authors use to help you see events in chronocological— chronological order, so for you to understand when events are happening, what order they're happening in. We have that term *BCE* again here: Before the Common Era. And then after year 1, it's Common Era. So we also have that abbreviation there. Can you find the Han dynasty? Oh, I see some of you putting your fingers on it. Nick, what years did the Han dynasty exist? Nick: Oh, 206 BCE to 221 CE.	• Ms. Hatt begins by directing students to notice the time span of the Han dynasty, and she reinforces the move that students are using: putting their fingers on the timeline.
Ms. H: Mm-hmm. And what can you learn from this timeline about the Han dynasty? Olivia, I'm really curious what you can learn from this timeline about the Han dynasty. Does it give you any information? What is it? What did you learn? Olivia: I guess it tells you how much they— I guess it tells you how long they ruled. Ms. H: That's true. You can get a sense of how long they were in power. McKenna, what else do you learn?	• Ms. Hatt affirms the response but asks what else the timeline shows.
McKenna: How long ago—like how long ago it was made or built. Ms. H: Mm-hmm. This timeline is really detailed, too, because in addition to the dates, there's more information. Can someone tell me about that? Kaleel, can you tell me about that? Is there— Yep, go ahead. Kaleel: No. Ms. H: Aveeni, can you help out? Aveeni: Yes. Ms. H: Listen carefully, Kaleel.	• McKenna refers again to the period of time, so Ms. Hatt draws attention to the information "in addition to the dates."
Aveeni: It says when China's dynasties in the Han part, it says wealthy, peaceful empire. So I was kind of right about my answer that I said about dynasty. It's wealthy because it says *Han* would mean—	• Aveeni shares information from the text on the timeline and her interpretation of it: wealthy and peaceful empire = "very nice place to live." *(continued)*

Video Episode 5.2: Making the Most of a Key Graphic *continued*	Our Notes
Ms. H: Han. [corrects pronunciation] Aveeni: —wealthy. *Han* would mean wealthy, peaceful empire. That would mean it's a very nice place to live— Ms. H: Yeah. Aveeni: —in the Han dynasty era. Ms. H: Mm-hmm. Lynn, do you have any more information? Lynn: I partially agree with Aveeni, partially disagree. 'Cause if the Han dynasty, just the t—the time when the Hans ruled, but it doesn't exactly mean wealthy, peaceful empire. It just means that that's—that it was the Han dynasty times. Ms. H: On the timeline, though, under— I think what Aveeni was looking at is that under where it says Han dynasty, it says that it was wealthy, peaceful empire. So it actually tells us those words. There's some more words there, too. Will you read those, Lynn? Lynn [reading]: "Buddhism emerges from India." Ms. H [reading]: "Buddhism [corrects pronunciation] emerges from India." Ms. H: Now this is a very complete timeline because usually you have some dates and events on them, but this one, Lynn, added a little bit of information, the most important information for you so that you could get a sense of that time period.	• Ms. Hatt presses for more information about the Han dynasty. • Lynn's comment indicates that she's still looking at the dates on the timeline rather than the information below it. • So Ms. Hatt specifically directs attention to the information "under where it says Han dynasty." • Ms. Hatt asks Lynn to read from that part of the timeline and reinforces the idea that the timeline is "very complete," providing dates and events plus other information.

Video Episode 5.3: Connecting Information From Multiple Sources

As you watch this video episode, notice how Ms. Hatt directs students to connect important information from multiple sources. Again, jot down your observations and then compare your notes with ours.

 5.3: **Connecting Information From Multiple Sources** (2:14)

Video Episode 5.3: Connecting Information From Multiple Sources	Our Notes
Ms. H: Before we move on, I want to know, how does all this information about the Han dynasty help us understand the building of these tombs and what was found in the tombs? I think the author has provided us a little bit of an explanation. McKenna? McKenna: That when they built the tombs, they try to make enough space for all of their—almost all of their belongings, like their vases and stuff, like all their vases and—and stuff like that. And the stuff in it, they— In Chi—in China, people believed that their soul—they—they live— They live after a person dies. So that's why they would [inaudible] the food and like their horse—their horse and chariot. Ms. H: Let's think about the Han dynasty. What do you know about the Han dynasty? Shawn? Shawn: That they were—that they got all the stuff and put it in the—in the tombs before they—like many years before they died. Ms. H: Uh-huh, but let's think about what's happening in the Han dynasty during that time. Like what's—what's it like? Student: It looks—it sounds like it's peaceful. Ms. H: Peaceful. What's another word that Aveeni used? Do you remember? Aveeni, what's another word you used to describe the Han dynasty? You said peaceful and— Aveeni: Wealthy. Ms. H: Wealthy. Does that—does that make sense? Shawn: *Wealthy* means like they're sort of rich. Ms. H: Uh-huh. So does that make sense for what was found in the tombs? Someone want to tell me more about that, explain that for us? Sydney? Sydney: Well, since they're rich, that explains why they have a lot of treasures in this tomb.	• After discussing the timeline on page 3, a student reads the paragraphs on the page. • Ms. Hatt's question invites students to connect the information about the Han dynasty—available from the text and the timeline—and the building and contents of the tombs. • Although McKenna's comment touches on the idea that the contents of the tomb relate to the beliefs of people in the Han dynasty, Ms. Hatt poses a question that focuses on what students know about what the Han dynasty was like. • Shawn responds but doesn't address the question, which Ms. Hatt poses once again, but in a more specific form. • When a student offers "peaceful," Ms. Hatt specifically refers to Aveeni's comments about the timeline information, and Aveeni again provides information about the wealth of the dynasty. • With that reminder, Sydney connects the valuable objects in the tomb with the wealth that was enjoyed during the Han dynasty—at least by the royalty.

Discussion Moves Demonstrated in the Video Episodes

We selected the video episodes that you viewed while reading this chapter to highlight the important discussion moves noted below.

- Video Episode 5.1: Collaborating to Build an Explanation
  - Invite students to contribute to developing an explanation and include your own contribution when needed.
- Video Episode 5.2: Making the Most of a Key Graphic
  - Identify key aspects of a graphic and be persistent in focusing students' attention on those aspects.
- Video Episode 5.3: Connecting Information From Multiple Sources
  - Direct students to connect information from different parts of a text.
  - Remind students to use information provided by relevant student comments.

Take It Away

Use the discussion plan for "Jade Burial Suits" with your students and capture the discussion on videotape or audiotape. Transcribe key moments in the discussion to analyze your discussion moves. Use the transcript analysis tools in Appendix A to guide your analysis.

CHAPTER 6

Contexts and Considerations for Text-Based Discussions

*I*n Chapters 2–5, we presented a template for looking closely at informational texts for the purpose of planning how to use discussion to support students in interpreting and learning from those texts. We applied that template to four sample texts and shared excerpts of teachers leading discussions of those texts with students in grades 4 and 6. In this chapter, we discuss other factors that influence the course of a text-based discussion, including the text selected, the orientation teachers bring to their role, and (in a related fashion) the classroom norms that are in place with respect to the roles of students and teachers. We conclude the chapter by reviewing lessons we learned as we prepared teachers to engage in text-based discussions. We begin, however, with a brief discussion of the contemporary educational context in the United States as it relates to the use of text-based discussion.

The Contemporary Educational Landscape in the United States

At the time that this volume was being prepared, 45 states in the United States had adopted the Common Core State Standards (CCSS). In a country in which the control of education has been highly localized and curricula decentralized, this move is a novel phenomenon. Whether the CCSS will have traction remains to be seen, but from the perspective of literacy educators, the standards are interesting in their own right. They represent the CCSS authors' best attempts to "backward map" toward readiness for the text demands associated with college and readiness for a career.

Consistent with our attention to discipline-specific goals when analyzing a text in the planning process, the CCSS target the teaching of disciplinary-specific literacy in the language arts, history/social studies, science, and technical subjects. Consistent with our focus on informational text, the CCSS recommend that over the course of students' school careers, the balance of opportunity shifts toward the reading of informational texts, such that by the last year of high school, students will be reading 70% informational text and 30% literary text. Consistent with our focus on the big ideas in a text, the CCSS call for close, attentive reading that leads to knowledge building with text—the knowledge building that happens when readers not only attend to what the text says explicitly but also engage in making logical inferences from the text. This anchor standard resonates with the heuristic we have proposed, which is that teachers view text-based discussions as the site in which teachers and students collaborate to create textual coherence and build robust mental representations of the text content.

Three of the anchor CCSS speak to the importance of attending to author's craft and text structure while reading by, for example, analyzing how specific word choices shape meaning or by analyzing how parts of the text (whether those are sentences, sections, or chapters) relate to one another and contribute to the text's meanings. This is consistent with our suggestion that teachers should evaluate texts to determine how the structure supports comprehension and knowledge building and how discussion can be used to cue students to these structural features.

Three of the anchor standards are specific to the integration of knowledge and ideas, a goal that can be achieved both within the reading of a single text and by reading and discussing two or more texts. We have not, in Chapters 2–5, addressed the topic of leading text-based discussions across multiple texts, although we appreciate the value that selecting texts that address similar themes/topics can play in supporting knowledge building. A casual online search reveals the interest that educators have in the development of "text sets," or the assembly of multiple texts—and genres of text—that are topically or thematically related. Often, what motivates the selection of the text set are issues of accessibility and interest—in other words, offering students an array of texts that represent different levels of complexity (see our discussion of text complexity below) and different means of communicating (e.g., through poetry, historical fiction, illustration, or diary). We argue that the same principles applied to the analysis of a single text could be used in the analysis of and planning with multiple texts, with the opportunity to examine the role of genre and structure becoming more prominent as students reference multiple texts.

The final anchor standard in the CCSS speaks to the range of reading and the level of text complexity that students encounter, with the goal that students will, in fact, leave school able to read and learn from complex texts. We return to the topic of text complexity below when we discuss the selection of texts for text-based discussions. In summary, our reading of the CCSS suggests that text-based discussions are an ideal pedagogical match with the expectations laid out by the CCSS; text-based discussions provide an optimal context in which teachers and students can share the close reading of complex texts.

We would be remiss in our survey of the contemporary educational landscape if we did not acknowledge the changing demographics of the K–12 population. Between 1988 and 2008, the population of white students enrolled in U.S. public schools decreased from 68% to 55% (U.S. Department of Education, 2009), whereas the population of other ethnic groups increased from 32% to 44% altogether, with Hispanic students comprising the majority (increasing from 6% to 21% in this time frame; Planty et al., 2009). Concomitant with these changes in demographics is the rapid growth of English learners (ELs) across the United States. In fact, the EL student population is the fastest growing group in the nation; in 2009, 21% of children ages 5–17 (or 11.2 million) spoke a language other than English at home (U.S. Department of Education, 2009).

We think that these figures elevate the importance of text-based discussions for the following reasons. The research of Lesaux, Rupp, and Siegel (2007) points to the striking similarity between ELs and native speakers of English in terms of the development of the foundational reading skills that are most commonly measured when examining reading achievement: letter identification, word reading accuracy, and word reading fluency. What sets apart ELs is that persistently low *language* skills compromise text comprehension, a view that is supported by other scholars who hypothesize that ELs struggle with comprehension because of the linguistic demands of academic text (Schleppegrell, 2001, 2004). In addition, Goldenberg and Coleman (2010) hypothesize that the poor performance of ELs on reading measures is related to their levels of background knowledge on the text topics. Each of these hypotheses speaks to the potential value of text-based discussions. In that context, ELs have the opportunity to hear and use language, learn vocabulary that is integral to understanding content, learn how language functions to make meaning, and build content knowledge. These are all features that have been identified as important to the teaching of ELs (August & Shanahan, 2006).

Selecting Texts for Text-Based Discussions

In this section, we consider what should guide teachers' decision making regarding the selection of texts for text-based discussions. The texts that we feature in this volume were commissioned specifically for our use. We made this choice to avoid copyright issues, but we also had other reasons. We wanted to work with texts that exhibited certain key features. We asked the authors to create texts that would be representative of the types of texts that students encounter in the upper elementary grades specific to content learning (in science and the social studies). We also asked that they be written to reflect discipline-specific features of content area texts; that is, texts about science topics often provide insight into how knowledge claims in science are generated, tested, and accepted, while social studies texts often provide insight into historical inquiry and the role of perspective in representing history.

We asked that the texts be typical with respect to their considerateness (Armbruster & Anderson, 1988); that is, they need to be representative of the types of texts that upper elementary students encounter in terms of structure, coherence, and audience appropriateness. Specifically, we asked the authors to prepare texts that provide a reason to have a text-based discussion. That is, they need to present ideas that are worth discussing *and* to provide opportunities for teachers and students to experience how a text-based discussion could serve to support students to construct a situation model of the ideas in the text. We also asked for texts that do not offer explicit coherence cues, include unfamiliar vocabulary, or present challenging graphics.

Our point is that the ideal text for independent reading is probably not the ideal text for a text-based discussion (see Mesmer, Cunningham, & Hiebert, 2012, for a comprehensive review of the features that contribute to text difficulty and text complexity). In fact, the presence of text complexity, which Mesmer et al. characterize in terms of vocabulary, syntax, and cohesion, is a desirable feature in selecting text that is worthy of discussion. We hope that the guidelines that we proposed to the authors will be helpful to teachers in making text selections. We also maintain that once teachers and their students have the experience of engaging in text-based discussions, it is possible for both the teachers and their students to nominate texts for classwide discussion or to stop and discuss particularly difficult and important parts of a text the class is reading.

The Teacher's Role in Text-Based Discussions

Discussion-based approaches to text comprehension are distinguished from the typical "elicitation, response, evaluation" pattern that has been criticized in the instructional literature to the extent that

(a) the discussion features open questions that invite multiple responses, (b) the teacher's responses are contingent upon the students' contributions to the discussion, and (c) there is the potential for a preponderance of student talk rather than teacher talk. Although students play a prominent role in text-based discussions, the discussions are largely directed by the teacher, who is posing meaning-based questions for the students to answer. As we argued in Chapters 2–5, the teachers' questions are shaped by the goals the teacher has identified for reading the text and by the text features the teacher anticipates to be challenging. This means that teachers must be knowledgeable about the content of the text, thoughtful about the kinds of questions that are likely to lead the students to deep understanding of the ideas, and capable of adjusting to students' needs and challenges as the discussion unfolds.

All of this is to say that the role of the teacher is quite prominent in text-based discussions. This consistent prominence is in contrast to "release of responsibility" models of instruction (Pearson & Gallagher, 1983), in which it is assumed that the learner is increasingly responsible for the cognitive activity, while the teacher plays a less major role. Although students who are consistently engaged in text-based discussions will assume more responsibility for their thinking over time, the teacher's role remains critical. We assume that teachers will select texts that increase in complexity; thus, each new text will present new opportunities and challenges.

Classroom Norms in Text-Based Discussions

While Kintsch's construction–integration model of reading has played a prominent role in our thinking about what happens in the mind of a reader while reading, the literature on the social aspects of learning has also been influential in our thinking about text-based discussions as a context for promoting sense making with text (Bransford, Brown, & Cocking, 1999). Contemporary views of classrooms as learning communities point to the importance of classroom norms that are designed to promote collaboration, the essence of which is the construction of shared meanings for conversations, concepts, and experiences (Roschelle, 1992). Given this definition, certain conditions are necessary to promote collaboration; one such condition is that the thinking is distributed among the members of the group and that all members of the group are sharing responsibility for the task at hand.

The process of learning to engage in collaborative learning is, in many respects, a process of creating a shared social world. For a teacher, this may well translate into cultivating new patterns of conversation in the classroom. Max Weinberg (the teacher whose text-based discussions were primarily featured in Chapter 2) characterized this process as he described how he prepares for text-based discussions:

> In my own classroom, I spend a considerable amount of time working on setting up the norms of TALK with my students. I teach students ways to show agreement, disagreement, ways to bring other people into a conversation, ways to build off one another's ideas in a conversation, ways to pull text evidence into a conversation and other pieces about tone of voice and body language....I remind students about respectfully engaging in talk about texts. (personal communication, September 13, 2012)

The outcomes of attending to these norms is revealed in a number of the video episodes of Ms. Hatt's classroom. These episodes were filmed in May, after students had participated in many other text-based discussions. In these episodes, it is not surprising to hear students referring to one another's ideas and explicitly building on those ideas: for example, "I agree with Shawn...,"

"Like Ariana said…, but I don't think…," and "I sort of am thinking like Mary, but I am sort of not thinking like Mary."

In one video episode that we selected for this chapter, we provide examples of the moves that Mr. Weinberg makes as he introduces the students to their first (to our knowledge) experiences with text-based discussions. In Episode 6.1.1, as he launches the discussion of "Black Death," Mr. Weinberg explicitly tells the students, "I'm the type of teacher that really loves to talk to students, and when I read with students, it really matters to me what you're thinking." Such a comment conveys his respect for students as informants and his expectation that, in fact, they are engaged in sense making. "But," Mr. Weinberg continues, "in order to really work well together, I want to share with you…the way we work together." Drawing from classroom rules that he sees posted on the wall, he builds on the norm of being responsible: "So, for 'be responsible,'…part of being a responsible student is that you're gonna think…you have to promise one another and me that you're gonna think…nod to show you promise." Mr. Weinberg introduces a second norm regarding listening carefully and then a third norm, being respectful, which he elaborates as "keeping your material still and your body as calm as possible." He then brings the conversation back around to "thinking, thinking, thinking, thinking.…Good members of a learning community are always ready to share their thinking."

In the second episode (6.1.2), Mr. Weinberg is debriefing about the previous day's text-based discussion before launching the discussion of "Coral Reefs." He acknowledges the "great thinking going on" in the classroom but then indicates that he wants to see broader participation by the students.

Ms. Hatt's launch of "Black Death" (video episode 6.4) is much less explicit, in terms of characterizing the norms that will prevail in this discussion, than Mr. Weinberg's and is testimony to the frequency with which she uses discussion in her class: "We're going to be doing what we usually do. We're going to be stopping, thinking, and talking about the information that the author gives us in order to understand it."

One challenge to the view of classroom discussion that we present above is class size; a large number of students in a class makes it difficult for all students to be heard in a discussion. One move that teachers make to accommodate large groups is to engage students in "turn and talk." Both of the teachers featured in this volume engage in this practice, with Mr. Weinberg using it more frequently. In video episode 6.2, we see him introducing a group of students to "turn and talk." What we found noteworthy in the excerpt is that before he even begins the discussion, he establishes who the talk partners will be; this struck us as a wise management move. Mr. Weinberg's use of "turn and talk" extends opportunities for all of the students to be engaged in the discussion. We noticed several features associated with his use of this practice: He poses a very specific issue/question for the students to discuss, he limits the time for "turn and talk" to two to three minutes, and he purposefully listens in to various groups during this time. In fact, in a 50-minute discussion in which there were three "turn and talk" episodes, he listened in on at least three-quarters of the pairs over the course of the period. Furthermore, he makes strategic use of ideas that he heard exchanged during "turn and talk" when the class returns for the whole-group discussion.

An additional feature of Mr. Weinberg's practice is demonstrated in video episode 6.3. On several occasions, we observed him listening in to the "turn and talk" of a student who had yet to make a contribution to the class discussion. Mr. Weinberg acknowledged the productive thinking he heard the student engage in and asked the student if he (typically) or she was willing to contribute that thinking to the class. If the student said no, Mr. Weinberg asked if he could present the student's idea. In every instance in which Mr. Weinberg began to share the student's idea, the student joined in and presented his or her own idea.

What About "Before, During, and After" Reading?

The reading community has a long tradition of thinking about reading lessons in terms of "before, during, and after" stages of reading a text. Our attention has been on the during stage, and we have proposed the close alignment of the during- and after-reading activities by suggesting that the exit activity be designed to provide evidence—to the teacher and to the students themselves—that the students successfully attained the conceptual goal(s) associated with the text selection. We have said less about the before stage of reading but want to point out the range of ways in which we designed the launch for each of our sample texts, a design decision that was shaped largely by the learning goals we identified for the reading.

Our launches ranged from the most simple—begin reading the text (in the case of "Black Death")—to the use of a video ("Coral Reefs"), to defining a key word in the title of the text (*harness* in "Harnessing the Wind"), to posing a scenario that would be analogous to the scenario students would be reading about ("Jade Burial Suits"). In each case, our choice was guided by the goal of activating a situation model closely related to the ideas in the text.

To elaborate, the first two paragraphs of "Black Death," in which the author shares the staggering figure about the incredible loss of life over such a brief period of time because of the spread of a disease, provide an immediate hook for the reader—a hook that can, in fact, serve as the launch for the discussion. In contrast, "Coral Reefs" begins with the description of a complex context that is unlikely to have been experienced by many students. Without a well-developed sense of this context, it would be difficult for students to make sense of the idea of an ecosystem and to think about the interdependence among living and nonliving organisms that characterizes an ecosystem. The word *harness* in the title "Harnessing the Wind" is key to making sense of the purpose of a wind turbine; hence, it makes sense to pause and ensure that students understand this key term. Finally, we chose the analogous scenario for "Jade Burial Suits" because engaging students in thinking about how archaeologists could use the artifacts that we will leave behind to make sense of our beliefs and values would position them to think about how the close study of the tombs and artifacts contained in those tombs was revealing something significant about the people of ancient China.

In short, we argue for flexibility in designing the before-reading activity, and we advocate for a pithy introduction that quickly gets students involved in the reading and discussion of the text. This is not to suggest that a teacher should not, at some point in time, provide direct and explicit vocabulary teaching. There is much evidence to suggest that vocabulary instruction is valuable, especially when it focuses on the teaching of academic vocabulary and when considering the needs of ELs, but we advise that this be designed and conducted as a separate activity.

Similarly, in the context of the discussion, we have found it most efficacious for the teacher to simply supply the meaning of an unfamiliar word rather than stop the flow of the discussion to engage in vocabulary development. There are, of course, exceptions; for example, in "Coral Reefs," understanding the phenomenon of coral bleaching is a key goal of the text. Students are likely to have encountered the word *bleach* in different contexts (e.g., bleaching one's clothes, bleaching one's teeth), and discussing the similarities can render the bleaching of coral more meaningful and memorable.

Managing the Scary Parts of Text-Based Discussions

When we have introduced preservice teachers to text-based discussions, naturally enough, the contingent nature of discussion is the most daunting. Student teachers are concerned that they won't know the next "right" question, or how to respond to a student whose comment seems to come out of left field, or what to do about the students who aren't contributing. We have learned a few lessons that seem worth sharing.

The first lesson will come as no surprise: the importance of planning. Teachers who have engaged in a thoughtful analysis of the text, have clear learning goals, have done research that extends their confidence with the conceptual content of the text, and have generated a set of initiating questions and planned the launch are at a distinct advantage when compared with those who think that they can engage in a reasonable text-based discussion in the moment. Namely, teachers who are well prepared have the cognitive space to attend to the contributions and responses of their students.

In addition to planning, there are other aspects of text-based discussions that can be supported by more knowledgeable others. In Appendix A, we provide a rubric that we developed for use with our own preservice teachers and refined in collaboration with other teacher educators. The rubric addresses the plan, the launch, the management of reader–text interactions, and the exit. Included in the rubric for the launch are a number of factors that are likely to be second nature to experienced teachers but may well elude preservice teachers, such as using one's voice to gain the attention of the students, maintaining eye contact with the students (as opposed to having one's eyes fixed on the text or plan), and pacing the discussion well so there's momentum. These aspects of general teaching practice will have fairly predictable and negative consequences if not attended to in the context of leading a discussion.

We have asserted that a powerful way to support teachers in learning to enact text-based discussions is to provide them with opportunities to practice, audiotape, selectively transcribe, and analyze their initial attempts. This is why we urge using the plans that are presented in Chapters 2–5. It has been our experience that teachers learn a great deal through enactment; for example, they are often surprised by what their analyses reveal. The most common realization that teachers make is that although they felt in the moment that the students were doing most of the talking, the fact is that they (the teachers) did most of the talking. A second realization is that— upon reflection and with the aid of transcripts—students typically *were* making sense, even if the teachers were unable to figure out, in the moment, what connection the student was making or what prompted the student's comment.

To end this chapter, we present several video episodes related to enacting text-based discussions, with particular attention to establishing and implementing discussion norms. Establishing participation structures and norms for sharing ideas allows teachers to facilitate discussions in powerful ways.

Viewing Video Episodes

We selected the following video episodes to demonstrate how Mr. Weinberg and Ms. Hatt prepare their students to engage in text-based discussions and facilitate their participation. As you watch each episode, jot down what you notice. Then, compare your notes with ours.

Video Episode 6.1.1: Establishing Norms for Discussion

 6.1.1: Establishing Norms for Discussion (3:02)

Video Episode 6.1.1: Establishing Norms for Discussion	Our Notes
Mr. W: I want to talk to you a little bit about the way I like to work when I'm with students. And I'm the type of teacher that really loves to talk to students, and when I read with students, it really matters to me what you're thinking. And that's what we're gonna be doing today is reading and sharing our thinking. But in order to really work well together, I want to share with you kind of what I share with my own students, the way we work together. So I know here at school you follow "Be safe, be responsible, and be respectful." Is that right? Do those sound familiar to you? Those are kind of like the school rules?	• We like the way Mr. Weinberg addresses students, sharing his love of talking with students, learning about their thinking, and engaging the class in sharing their thinking.
Mr. W.: So I was thinking wh—about the work we're doing today, and I stretched those out a little bit. So for "be responsible," this is what it means to me, and I hope you—you'll agree with these things for today that part of being a responsible student is that you're gonna think. And what I mean when I say "think" is think about the text that we're going to read. It's really interesting. There's a lot of cool stuff to look at and learn about. So, you have to promise one another and me that you're gonna think. Does everyone agree to promise that? You just nod to show you promise. Thanks. OK. "Listen carefully," or listen—careful listening, this should say. Let me add "listen carefully." Listen carefully, so if anyone's talking, like right now I'm talking and I see you're all looking at me, and I really appreciate that, I think you're listening really carefully. And then "share your thinking." So, part of being responsible and being like a good community member means that you're gonna share your—all that thinking you're doing, you'll be ready to share it.	• He follows his message up with specifics, building on a set of norms that students are familiar with and to which they are already held accountable. • We appreciate the enthusiasm that Mr. Weinberg shares with students.
Mr. W: Now it gets tricky 'cause we can't talk over one another, but just be prepared to share your thinking. Let me ask you a question. Is it OK as part of your own thinking to ask a question? What do you think? What do you think?	
Student: Yeah.	*(continued)*

Video Episode 6.1.1: Establishing Norms for Discussion *continued*	Our Notes
Mr. W: Yes. So, if you're not sure about something that I ask you, or you're wondering about something we read about, that's part of thinking, too. OK? Next, for "being respectful," I really ask you to respect me and respect one another by keeping your material still and your body as calm as possible. Hopefully you got a good night's rest. Hopefully you got to get a little bit of exercise this morning on your way into school so you'll be able to really be calm, right? Mr. W: And then your hands down when someone is speaking. I know sometimes when I'm sitting in a chair listening to a teacher teach, I can't stop thinking about my own thought, and I just—I keep waving my hand. And then I realize that's probably distracting the person next to me. So if I'm talking, or one of your classmates is talking, if you can j— even if you really want to share your thinking, if you can keep your hand down, that'd be great. Can we agree to that, too? OK. And then just be ready to share your thinking. Part of being respectful is you're always ready. You see how this keeps popping up? Thinking, thinking, thinking, thinking. Really good citizens, right? Good members of a learning community are always ready to share their thinking.	

Video Episode 6.1.2: Revising Norms for Discussion

 6.1.2: Revising Norms for Discussion (0:50)

Video Episode 6.1.2: Revising Norms for Discussion	Our Notes
Mr. W: Today we're gonna be reading about something totally different and having a discussion about it. I know yesterday we reviewed the rules about being responsible and being respectful. You did a great job with that yesterday. You were really respectful. You really held on to your materials. You really listened carefully to me and to one another. I'm hoping that today we can have a little bit more of a discussion. And what I mean by that is not just that the same people keep talking, but that more and more people feel comfortable sharing their ideas with all of us 'cause that's really why I came, to talk to you and to hear your ideas about these topics that we're reading about. Does that s—can we agree to that?	• We notice the specificity with which Mr. Weinberg provides students with feedback about the participation in the previous day's discussion. • Mr. Weinberg ups the ante now, to the extent that he hopes to hear from more students. *(continued)*

Video Episode 6.1.2: **Revising Norms for Discussion** *continued*	**Our Notes**
Students: Yeah. Mr. W: You're all really—you're, you're great. You're all really, really well behaved and respectful, so I know that you've got great thinking going on, and I want to make sure that we get a chance to hear that. And I'm glad we have some new faces today, too.	

Video Episode 6.2: Introducing "Turn and Talk"

 6.2: Introducing "Turn and Talk" (1:09)

Video Episode 6.2: **Introducing "Turn and Talk"**	**Our Notes**
Mr. W: I really want you—when it's time, when it's appropriate—to feel comfortable sharing your thinking. And thinking can be thoughts you're having about the text, or a question that you're having about the text, or even a question if you're just confused about what we're reading. So one way you might talk is if I call on you, you can raise your hand. You can raise your hand, and then I'll call on you, or I might have you turn and talk to someone sitting right next to you. And just to make it easy, as I ask you to turn and talk, I—when I say go, I want everyone to make eye contact with someone sitting next to you and kind of give 'em a nod to mean you're gonna be the person I talk to. Doesn't have to be your best friend, and we could probably do this really easily. If Jessica and Michaela are sitting next to each other, would it make much sense for them to be partners when we talk? [Although these students are seated next to each other, they both have another student sitting on the other side of them.] Student: No. Mr. W: Even if they're buddies, because we have four people here. So, just think—look at your row and think about who it makes most sense to talk to. Make eye contact and just give a quick nod. Go. Perfect. Perfect. Perfect. Perfect. Perfect. Perfect. Thank you. OK. Looked really good.	• In this exchange, Mr. Weinberg clarifies the different kinds of thinking that students can share. • We noticed that Mr. Weinberg anticipates what could become a management issue—choosing a partner—and resolves this matter before it becomes a problem.

Video Episode 6.3: Extending "Turn and Talk" Into the Discussion

 6.3: Extending "Turn and Talk" Into the Discussion (5:08)

Video Episode 6.3: Extending "Turn and Talk" Into the Discussion	Our Notes
Mr. W: I wanted to talk about something. I think Jonathon brought this up with *theories*. Did you all—had you all heard the word—you can just nod or quietly say yes—had you heard the word *theories* before?	
Student: No.	
Student: Yes.	
Mr. W: Theories? And, and I'm glad we're—we're in this room [the science classroom] because I bet you all know that scientists come up with theories. You get a little bit—you get some ideas from little pieces of evidence, and you piece together a theory, and then you test it out. Well, first, did you know that there are people who make a living out of studying history who are called historians? You knew that? Yeah. That's th—that's what they do for a living.	• Mr. Weinberg connects the theory building that scientists do with the theorizing of historians. This is an interesting move because it seems more likely that students will have encountered theorizing in their study of science than in their study of history.
Mr. W: Well, historians, people who study history, also come up with theories. They get little bits of pieces of information, they come up with a theory, and then they go and try to prove it. Did you hear anything in this—from what we've read on pages 2 and 3, really—about how the historians provided their theory about the travel of this disease? Do you have anything that shows proof about their theory? Let's look back at the top of page 3. [reading] "Within days, Sicilians began to come down with the disease. Before long, the Black Death reached other cities along the Mediterranean coast. Historical documents record that the disease spread inland with terrifying speed." What are historical documents? Very quickly, turn to the person next to you and talk about what you think it means when they say "historical documents."	• This is a rich part of the text, and it lends itself to "turn and talk." There is no explicit information about the artifacts and historical documents that historians might work with; hence, it is a particularly opportune time for students to explore the idea together and generate ideas about what might have been available to support historians' theory building.
[The student pairs talk to each other, and Mr. Weinberg checks in with some students.]	
Mr. W: And while you're talking, see if you can name some examples of what might a historical document be.	
[Mr. Weinberg continues checking in with various students.]	*(continued)*

Video Episode 6.3: Extending "Turn and Talk" Into the Discussion *continued*	Our Notes
Mr. W: Would like—would a video be a historical document? It kinda could be, right? Do you think in 1930, in 1347, they had videos? No. How about like a letter?	
Students: Yeah.	
Mr. W: What about if they buried people and had to fill out like some paperwork to show that they were buried in a cemetery? Could that be [inaudible]? What else? Erin, what are you thinking about?	
Erin: [inaudible]	
Mr. W: Like what? Like give an example of one.	
Student: [inaudible]	
Mr. W: That's good.	
Student: [inaudible]	
Mr. W: That's good. That would be proof, right? To study their body and their DNA, like their—whatever things they can find in their bones. OK. OK.	
Mr. W: OK. What'd you come up with? Yes, Alonna?	
Alonna: We came up with like—like a document like [inaudible].	
Student: Like a document's like a piece of paper that you study. Like it's history 'cause it's a historical document.	
Mr. W: Good. So, a piece of paper can be a document. What do you imagine would be written on that piece of paper? What kind of information?	• We think it is important that Mr. Weinberg probes the students' responses; "a piece of paper" is quite vague.
Student: Historical information?	
Mr. W: Historical, so it's something back in time around 1347. Maybe like someone back there in the—in the back row said like maybe a birth record or a record of someone dying. Someone else had a—or someone being buried. Did someone else have another idea? Adam, did you want to say something? Go ahead.	• Here, Mr. Weinberg draws on information he heard from two student pairs during "turn and talk."
Adam: It could be a monument.	
Mr. W: A monument would be good. Say more about that. What do you picture th—being on the monument?	• Again, we notice how Mr. Weinberg probes students' thinking about the information that would appear on a document that would serve as historical evidence.
Student: It could be like a historical monu—monument, and—and it would say something about the person, like a statue or something.	
Mr. W: So, a statue or a headstone in a—in a cemetery that said like when people lived?	

(continued)

Video Episode 6.3: Extending "Turn and Talk" Into the Discussion *continued*	Our Notes
Student: When people were—when people—how old they were, when they lived, what their name was, also what their last name was, and when they died. Mr. W: OK. So, there are historical documents, like the ones that have been mentioned, and all of these historical documents show that this disease spread with terrifying speed, so fast, so rapidly. So, historians created this theory that this must have been an awful plague, something that came on very quickly and spread so fast. OK, let's keep reading in the middle of page 3.	• Mr. Weinberg ties this part of the discussion together by bringing the talk back to the idea of a theory and the role that historical documents played in building a theory regarding the spread of the Black Death.

Video Episode 6.4: Reintroducing a Familiar Pattern of Classroom Discussion

 6.4: Reintroducing a Familiar Pattern of Classroom Discussion (1:10)

Video Episode 6.4: Reintroducing a Familiar Pattern of Classroom Discussion	Our Notes
Ms. H: Readers, today we are going to be looking at a text together. And we're going to be doing what we usually do. We're going to be stopping, thinking, and talking about the information that the author gives us in order to understand it. The text you have in front of you is going to give you a sequence of events that happened more than 750 years ago. That's a long time ago. And so, 750 years ago, things were different. Technology was different, information was different, resources were different, and so people acted and thought differently than how we might think today. And so, I want you to keep that in mind as we're reading, because remember, the events took place 750 years ago. You have a text in front of you. Like I said, we're gonna read it together. I'm going to begin reading, and sometimes I may ask for your contribution, and you can volunteer to read if that's what you would like to do.	• The history that Ms. Hatt has with this class is apparent in this exchange. She assumes that the students are quite familiar with the use of discussion to talk about the ideas in a text.

Video Episode 6.5: Looking Closely at a Discussion Launch

 6.5: Looking Closely at a Discussion Launch (5:15)

Video Episode 6.5: Looking Closely at a Discussion Launch	Our Notes
Ms. Hatt: This article that we will be reading is about discoveries that were made in China. I'm going to show you where China is on the map. There's actually a pushpin on it. We're gonna start by taking a look at the photographs that the author incl— included for you on the front page. I'm going to read the captions, and you look closely so that we can discuss them. I'm gonna start with the one at the top. The captions say, [reading] "The burial suit of Prince Liu Sheng." The picture on the bottom says, "Princess Dou Wan's burial suit." What do you see in these photographs? Mary, what do you see? Mary: That there was—there's a little—like there's some kind of ledge that is holding a burial suit. And I have a question. What's a burial suit? Ms. H: Well, that's one of the things that we're going to find out in this text. Do you kind of have an idea of what a burial suit might be, Mary? Mary: Yeah, sort of. Ms. H: Can you ex—can you tell us? Mary: Yeah, that it might be like something that you go in when you— Like—maybe you like—like when— Now—like now usually they'll get you something that like you just take one of those big—those black—the coffins. Ms. H: Uh-huh. Mary: And maybe in the olden days for important people, they would have used—like they may have like used [inaudible]. Ms. H: OK. What do you think about that, Cassidy? Cassidy: I think that a burial suit is kind of like a tomb. Ms. H: OK. Shawn? Shawn: I know a lot about Egyptians, and I know that they had sort of burial suits. And so, I'm guessing that this is gonna be for like dead people. That like it puts their body in, then is covered up. Ms. H: Hmm. Aveeni, what do you think?	• We were struck by the amount of eliciting of students' ideas that Ms. Hatt engages in as she launches the reading and discussion of "Jade Burial Suits." • In the following exchange, there are at least eight students contributing their ideas about what these pictures and "jade burial suits" could possibly refer to. *(continued)*

Video Episode 6.5: Looking Closely at a Discussion Launch *continued*	Our Notes
Aveeni: I'd like to build on Mary and Shawn's idea. It's prob—it's kind of like in Egypt where they have the mummies, and they put the mummy's things in their bodies, but it's not actually a burial suit. But I think a burial suit is something like they— They probably after they die, they preserve them, and they probably kind of put them in there. And then they have them shaped the way they kind of look like, how they are in real life or how they did look like when they were alive, how they were shaped. And then they put the stuff on them, and then they were shaped into that form. And then they probably did something to them so it could dry off or make it freeze so it could make it not move around so much.	
Ms. H: Sounds like many of you have some background knowledge, or some connections, that you're making to this topic. And it's important for us to remember those so that once we read the information, we can decide if we were accurate or if there's some adjustm—adjustments we need to make in our thinking. Maria?	
Maria: I think a burial suit is something that they put on a dead person before they bury them and—so that they won't like get—like they won't dis—decompose or anything, instead of putting them in like a casket or something.	
Ms. H: OK. Let's look at the photographs again. What do you see here in the photographs? You might have to look really closely. Kaleel, what do you see?	• Ms. Hatt redirects students to the photographs.
Kaleel: It looks like iron or metal.	
Ms. H: Mm-hmm. And Darrell?	
Darrell: I see that this suit in—with the guy in it is in this tomblike structure.	
Ms. H: OK. Olivia?	
Olivia: I disagree with Kaleel because it said "jade burial suits."	
Ms. H: Tell me more.	• It appears that Ms. Hatt sustains the exchange by offering very few comments regarding the students' contributions. She simply encourages with questions such as "What do you think?" or with a comment such as "Tell me more."
Olivia: I think jade is like one of those kind of stones and jewels that are k—actually precious. And they're actually green, too, and smooth.	
Ms. H: OK. Go ahead, Sydney .	
Sydney: I'm gonna add on to Olivia's. I think the burial suit was made with jade tiles.	
Ms. H: Hmm. Those do look a little bit like tiles, huh? OK, Shawn.	*(continued)*

Video Episode 6.5: Looking Closely at a Discussion Launch *continued*	Our Notes
Shawn: I agree with Olivia and Sydney. And what I'm gonna add on is I think that th— I think that they—like they put it sort of like it's a suit of armor. Ms. H: That's an interesting idea. Shawn: 'Cause it looks like the face has a mask on it. Ms. H: Aveeni? Aveeni: I agree with Sydney and Olivia, but I kind of disagree with Shawn because I see— I'm looking at this picture, and I have no idea how this would be a little bit of armor. I think it might be able to protect them or something from—from spiders and stuff, but I don't think it would be like stuff like swords and stuff. Ms. H: Well, let's jump into the text. It's a little bit longer, so we wanna get started.	

Take It Away

We hope that this chapter and the others have evoked a generous response from you, a response that will influence your enthusiasm for planning and enacting text-based discussions. We hope that you will have opportunities to explore the ideas in this book in teacher study groups, professional development workshops, or teacher education courses. We know from experience that developing the specialized knowledge that informs the enactment of text-based discussions is the result of a willingness to engage in and reflect on such discussions over and over again.

Our attention to planning—one might say our obsession with planning—speaks to our belief that planning is key to the process of leading text-based discussions. As we suggested earlier, planning enables teachers to identify the destination, map a course likely to get the group to that destination, and identify the resources in the text that will support that journey. There is, in fact, a solid literature with a rich history speaking to the importance of teacher planning in predicting student learning opportunities (Wittrock, 1986).

But we also want to emphasize that planning is not the same as enacting or engaging in a discussion. That is, although thorough planning is critical, so too is the ability to be attentive and responsive to how students respond and offer their thoughts and questions during a discussion. It has been our experience that knowing a text well, being familiar with its features and content, allows teachers to be attentive and responsive, mindful of what their students are saying and what those comments reveal about students' understanding or confusion. This notion of responsiveness between teachers and students has been described in various ways: dialogic teaching (Alexander, 2006; Boyd & Markarian, 2011; Nystrand, 1997), thoughtfully adaptive instruction (Boyd, 2012; Duffy & Hoffman, 1999), and negotiated instruction (Pica, 1994; Van Den Branden, 2000). According to Boyd,

> Effective teachers are those who plan engaging and challenging lessons, but then, in the act of teaching, are responsive to student cues....They exercise professional judgment, pedagogical expertise, and

flexibility as they consider what students contribute, anchor their questioning in student contributions, and provide necessary support with the questions they ask—support that bridges to an appropriate learning or teaching purpose. (p. 26)

In this, our final "Take It Away," we hope that you take away what you've learned from engaging with the ideas in this book, and what you anticipate learning as you plan and enact text-based discussions in your classroom. We also hope that your experiences will enrich your teaching and thinking and support the learning of your students.

APPENDIX A

Transcript Analysis Tools

This appendix includes tools for analyzing discussion transcripts and videotapes of discussions and for conducting observations of discussions. There are three tools: the Transcript Coding Manual, the Discussion Competence Continuum, and the Discussion Episode: Take 2. We suggest that the coding manual be used by teachers for an initial analysis of their transcripts—that is, before teachers have been introduced to the ideas about text-based discussion presented in this book. We suggest that teachers and coaches use the competence continuum to analyze transcripts and videotapes and also as an observation tool. The discussion episode rerun activity is useful for teachers, coaches, and teacher educators.

Each tool requires that a discussion be videotaped or audiotaped and then transcribed. The transcribing process can be time-consuming, but teachers have testified to the importance of completing the task. As one teacher noted,

> That is why transcribing these [discussions] is so vital. You feel it as you're typing it in. You're hearing it. And you see it as it comes up on the screen....You've got to see it, you've got to touch it, you've got to hear it, to know to change. (Kucan, 2007, p. 228)

In the sections that follow, we describe each of these three tools in turn.

Transcript Coding Manual

The Transcript Coding Manual is a tool for analyzing transcripts of discussions by focusing on the kinds of questions teachers pose and the kinds of responses teachers make to students. Using the coding manual involves labeling each question and response in a transcript and then organizing the information into tables. The kinds of questions and responses included in the coding manual are those that we have found teachers use most frequently. There are other kinds of questions and responses, and teachers can modify the coding manual to include those.

Questions

Kind of Question	Explanation	Example
Retrieve	The teacher asks the students to remember or locate information explicitly stated in a text or represented in the text's illustrations.	• Where is Vinalhaven?
Relate	The teacher asks the students to think and talk about personal experiences and/or offer personal opinions or reactions.	• Have you ever seen a wind turbine? • Would you want to live near a wind farm?
Explain	The teacher asks the students to focus on explaining the meaning of a specific text segment or idea.	• What does the wind turbine have to do with electricity?
Infer	The teacher asks the students to consider information from more than one text segment or to read between the lines in a single text segment in order to figure out why something happened.	• Why do you think so many people voted to build the wind turbines on Vinalhaven?
Predict	The teacher asks the students to consider text information to figure out what might happen next or what might result from an action.	• Based on the experiences of the citizens of Vinalhaven, do you think they would recommend building wind turbines in other communities?
Connect/compare/contrast	The teacher asks the students to compare, contrast, or connect information from one part of the text to information in another part.	• Compare the advantages of using wind turbines with their disadvantages.
Evaluate	The teacher asks the students to provide an evaluation of or judgment about a situation described in the text or to choose among possible alternatives.	• If you were on a team investigating the use of wind turbines, what would you recommend in your report?

Responses

Kind of Response	Explanation	Examples
Collect	The teacher repeats/rephrases the question to the same or a different student.	• Who has another idea? • Who found another example?
Probe	The teacher requests additional information, such as a reason or evidence for a student's response.	• What makes you say that? • What evidence supports your idea?
Connect	The teacher elicits responses that connect to a previous student response by asking the students if they agree or disagree or if they want to add on to what another student said.	• What do you think of Amy's idea? • Amy has given us some important information to think about. What else do we need to consider?

After labeling transcript questions and responses, teachers can organize their counts into tables, such as the ones below.

Kind of Question	(Number of Times)/(Total Number of Questions) = Percentage
Retrieve	
Relate	
Explain	
Infer	
Predict	
Connect/compare/contrast	
Evaluate	

Kind of Response	(Number of Times)/(Total Number of Responses) = Percentage
Collect	
Probe	
Connect	

Another informative analysis of a transcript involves teachers simply counting the number of lines in a transcript that are spoken by themselves and by their students. The result of such a count is an important indication about the relative contributions to the discussion made by the participants.

	Number of Lines	Percentage
Teacher talk		
Student talk		

To calculate the percentage of teacher talk and student talk,

- Divide the number of lines of teacher talk by the total number of lines of talk.
- Divide the number of lines of student talk by the total number of lines of talk

Discussion Competence Continuum

The Discussion Competence Continuum is a tool that assesses aspects of text-based discussion presented in this book via four rubrics: the discussion plan, the launch, reader–text interactions, and the exit. The continuum provides an analytic framework for talking about a text-based discussion and for measuring progress in enacting such discussions.

Rubric for Assessing the Plan

Competence Continuum →

1	2	3
The text is not a good selection for the students: It may be too difficult, not sufficiently challenging, or not rich enough to support a discussion.	There are some aspects of the text that lend themselves to a text-based discussion, but overall this is not the case.	The text is an appropriate selection for the students.
There are identified learning goals, but they are not clear, are not sufficiently specific, and/or do not reflect the big ideas of the text.	The identified learning goals are clear and specific; they generally, but not completely, reflect the big ideas of the text.	The identified learning goals are clear, specific, and reflect the big ideas of the text.
The text is not segmented in a way that will promote building understanding of the text; the text segments are too large (leading to too few opportunities) or too small (providing too little information to think about).	There are good examples of segmenting the text appropriately, but the segmenting is not consistent.	There is consistent use of productive segmenting of the text.
Few of the planned questions are supportive of learning goals, few take advantage of the text features, or few invite a deep interaction with the text.	Some of the planned questions are generally supportive of learning goals, some take advantage of the text features, and some invite a deep interaction with the text.	The planned questions are consistently supportive of learning goals, take advantage of text features, and invite a deep interaction with the text.

Rubric for Assessing the Launch

Competence Continuum →

1	2	3
The teacher does not articulate clearly, speak at an appropriate rate, project his or her voice well, make eye contact with the students, nor use their names.	The teacher articulates clearly, at an appropriate rate, and with adequate projection, but not consistently. Occasionally, but consistently, the teacher makes good eye contact with the students and uses their names.	The teacher consistently articulates clearly, at an appropriate rate, and with adequate projection, making good eye contact with the students and using their names.
The teacher does not identify the purpose nor the structure (e.g., the roles and responsibilities that the students will assume) of the discussion.	The teacher identifies the purpose or the structure, but not both.	The teacher identifies both the purpose and the structure.
The teacher demonstrates a less than ideal use of time, lingers too long with the introduction (of themselves, of the topic, of the learning goals, or in the act of eliciting prior knowledge), or moves too quickly into the interaction.	The teacher accomplishes a subset (but not the complete set) of the following: setting the purpose, identifying the goals, and eliciting the students' prior knowledge.	The teacher uses time well and progresses at a good pace to set the purpose, identify the goals, and elicit the students' prior knowledge.
The launching question/comment/activity is not a good match with the content, nor does it take advantage of the prior discussion with the class.	The launching question/comment/activity is a good match with the content but does not incorporate the prior discussion with the class.	The launching question/comment/activity is a good match with the content and takes advantage of the content and the prior class discussion.

Rubric for Assessing Reader–Text Interactions

Competence Continuum →

1	2	3
The teacher demonstrates a number of difficulties related to classroom management; such as handling disruptions, engaging the reluctant talker, and dealing with domineering talkers.	The teacher demonstrates the use of productive classroom management strategies in dealing with some types or some instances of classroom management difficulty.	The teacher consistently demonstrates productive classroom management.
The teacher calls only on students who are bidding for a turn and likely to make helpful contributions with little support.	The teacher calls only on students who are bidding for a turn.	The teacher attends to turn taking across the whole group of students.
The teacher overrelies on planned questions, leading to inflexibility in the discussion.	The teacher demonstrates some flexibility with using planned questions.	The teacher makes flexible use of questions and demonstrates an ability to improvise.
The teacher asks questions that are too general, not aligned with the learning goals, or not cohesive.	The teacher occasionally uses a line of questions that are tailored to the text and the discussion, are aligned with the learning goals, and cohere.	The teacher consistently uses a line of questions that are tailored to the text and the discussion, are aligned with the learning goals, and cohere.
The teacher consistently answers his or her own questions when students don't respond, rather than reformulating the question or providing enough wait time.	The teacher occasionally answers his or her own questions when students don't respond.	The teacher skillfully reformulates questions and uses wait time when students don't respond to the initial question.
The teacher engages in serial questioning, failing to use student contributions to advance the discussion.	The teacher begins to show evidence of uptake, occasionally using student contributions.	The teacher engages in uptake of student talk by associating ideas with students who offered those ideas, linking student contributions, weaving student contributions into the questions, and exploring students' responses.
The teacher fails to follow up on students' responses for the purpose of clarifying or extending their thinking.	The teacher occasionally follows up on students' responses for the purpose of clarifying or extending student thinking.	The teacher appropriately probes students' responses for the purpose of clarifying or extending student thinking.
The teacher reveals superficial knowledge of the text content, which prohibits productive interactions.	The teacher demonstrates familiarity with parts, but not all, of the text.	Throughout the discussion, the teacher demonstrates a high degree of familiarity with the text content, which supports flexible questioning and responding.

Rubric for Assessing the Exit

Competence Continuum →

1	2	3
The teacher does not allocate time for the exit.	—	The teacher provides adequate time to wrap up the discussion in a purposeful manner.
The teacher does no "looking back."	The teacher makes only a superficial attempt to summarize or synthesize the discussion.	The teacher uses the exit to summarize, synthesize, and/or address misconceptions.
Even when appropriate, the teacher does no "looking ahead."	The teacher may refer to future learning or a future activity, but not in a precise or focused way.	The teacher links the text-based discussion to further learning or a future activity.
The teacher provides no opportunity for assessment (informal or formal).	The teacher provides an assessment opportunity that does not link optimally with the learning goals or the prior class discussion.	The teacher uses one of a repertoire of approaches to assess student learning (e.g., a quick-write in response to a question or prompt, "turn and talk," whole-group discussion, a small group listing the main points of the prior discussion on chart paper).

Discussion Episode: Take 2

In Chapters 4 and 5, we shared several examples of our initial attempts (take 1) and then our second attempts (take 2), and sometimes even more attempts (takes 3 and 4), in selecting learning goals and designing launches and exits. We have found that a similar approach is useful for analyzing specific episodes from a discussion transcript. The approach is simple: Teachers select an episode from their transcripts (take 1) and then create a revised version of the episode (take 2).

To create the revised version of the episode, teachers consider what discussion moves might have made the episode more supportive of student comprehension. Referring to the discussion moves presented in the summary of Chapters 2–5, teachers can select specific moves that might have promoted student thinking, understanding, and engagement. We have found that such reflective analysis provides teachers with specific examples of how they can continue to improve their enactments of text-based discussions.

The purpose of all three tools described here is to promote the kind of reflection and analysis that will support teachers in developing and deepening their specialized knowledge for planning and enacting text-based discussions.

APPENDIX B

Discussion Moves

*T*his appendix provides a summary of all the discussion moves used in this book. As we have explained, the purpose of the discussion moves is to support students in comprehending text information. Comprehension involves developing a situation model of the text information and organizing the information into a coherent mental representation. Discussion moves can mediate that process. We sort them into categories based on their goal: (a) to build coherence, (b) to scaffold comprehension, (c) to focus attention on text features, and (d) to make it real. These are explained in the sections below.

Build Coherence

- *Provide an initial framework for thinking about the text:* Posting questions about a text can guide students' thinking about the text before reading and can be used to summarize learning after reading. An example is in the discussion plan for "Coral Reefs." An introductory scenario can provide students with a framework for thinking about important text content. For example, the mud-covered school scenario in the discussion plan for "Jade Burial Suits" sets students up to think about the work of archaeologists in investigating artifacts found at a site.

- *Use tables, charts, and other graphic organizers to sort and connect text information:* Examples of this move can be found in the discussion plans for "Harnessing the Wind," "Black Death," and "Coral Reefs."

- *Provide verbal frameworks to organize student thinking and comments:* For example, in the discussion plan for "Coral Reefs," we asked students to compare and contrast information, or identify similarities and differences.

- *Cue students to connect related information from across a text:* For example, in the discussion plan for "Coral Reefs," we pointed out and asked students to connect the references to sunlight and shallow water, which appeared on pages 1, 2, and 3 of the sample text.

- *Ask students to connect textual and graphic sources of information in a text:* In the discussion plan for "Jade Burial Suits," we directed the students to connect the information in the timeline to the information in the text to make sense of why people stopped creating jade burial suits.

- *Consistently make use of key terms and concepts to anchor student thinking:* In the discussion plan for "Harnessing the Wind," we consistently referred to pros and cons. In the discussion plan for "Black Death," we introduced the notion of theory and defined it as "a working idea or an explanation that takes into account the available information." We explained that historians develop theories. We also used the word *theory* when we asked students to consider what theories people might have had to explain the treatments that they developed to prevent or cure the Black Death. In the discussion plan for "Coral Reefs," we consistently referred to *ecosystem* and *interdependence*. We also consistently made use of the key terms *causal chain, chain, links, link, events,* and *connected* in eliciting student thinking related to "Black Death." These consistent references keep students focused on the important ideas in the text.

- *Avoid digressions:* When appropriate, skip sections of the text that might divert students' attention from the important content. We did that in the discussion plans for "Harnessing the Wind" and "Jade Burial Suits."

Scaffold Comprehension

- *Engage students in explaining text information:* In all of the discussion plans, we asked students to explain their understanding of text information. In the process of developing an explanation, students connect information and organize it.

- *Press students to provide evidence for their ideas:* Both Ms. Hatt and Mr. Weinberg provided examples of pressing students to provide evidence for their ideas. Sometimes this involves asking students to find information in the text to support their claims.

- *Return to the text:* Asking students to return to the text to locate specific information or to reread information is an important move for refocusing student attention on what is important to think about.

- *Supply information when needed:* In some cases, a text may not provide enough information for students to use in building an understanding of it. In such cases, it is important to cue students to that fact. For example, in "Harnessing the Wind," we acknowledged the very general level of information in the section about how wind turbines work by saying, "The important idea here is...." We used this same move when referring to the diagram of the wind turbine by saying, "There's more to wind turbines than what is shown here...." At other times, some additional information can be provided to support student understanding. For example, in the discussion plan for "Jade Burial Suits," we anticipated that students would relate the Chinese tombs to Egyptian tombs and provided information about that relationship. We also provided information about the Silk Road that was not included in the text.

- *Acknowledge student contributions:* Let students know that their contributions are valuable by acknowledging their ideas and incorporating them into a collaboratively developed explanation. This move is apparent in the video episodes featuring both Mr. Weinberg and Ms. Hatt.

- *Revoice student contributions:* Because students are developing their understandings during a discussion, it is often the case that they struggle to express their ideas in coherent ways. To support their efforts, it is important to listen carefully to their contributions and to help them in organizing their ideas. Paraphrasing their comments and selecting the most relevant part of their comments to focus on are two ways to revoice student contributions. Revoicing sends a message to students that their thinking is developing and that their efforts are valued.

Focus Attention on Text Features

- *Draw attention to specific phrases and sentences:* In the discussion plan for "Harnessing the Wind," we used this move when we asked students to provide another way of saying "Despite these concerns," and again at the end of the discussion when we focused student attention on the sentence "Before long, there will be wind turbines in practically every part of the world." Selecting specific phrases or sentences and asking for interpretations sends a message about the importance of attending to that level of information in the text.

- *Focus attention on language cues:* In the discussion plan for "Harnessing the Wind," we pointed out the use of the contrastive connectives *however*, *despite*, and *but*. In the "Coral Reefs" plan, we focused on the use of multiple referents to describe the coral reef ecosystem.

- *Focus attention on word choice:* In the "Black Death" discussion plan, we drew students' attention to the words *think*, *believe*, and *confirm* and discussed the degree of certainty that each conveys.

- *Ask students to notice paragraph conventions:* In the discussion plan for "Coral Reefs," we directed students' attention to the topic sentences in two paragraphs and explained how those sentences cue readers about what to expect when reading the paragraphs.

Make It Real

- *Use maps and globes to locate places or routes mentioned in the text:* For example, in the discussion plan for "Jade Burial Suits," we used a world map to locate China and to trace the Silk Road.

- *Provide props:* In the plan for "Black Death," we suggested the use of a paper chain to represent the causal chain linking the germ *Yersinia pestis* to the events leading to the death of so many people in Europe.

- *Use realia:* If possible, provide hands-on examples of items mentioned in a text, such as the jade in "Jade Burial Suits."

- *Compare text information to situations that students are familiar with:* For example, in the "Jade Burial Suits" plan, we included a suggestion for comparing the size of the tomb in the illustration with the size of your classroom.

- *Use visual representations:* Asking students to use gestures or create sketches can support their understanding of text information. For example, in the discussion plan for "Coral Reefs," we suggested that students use their hands to portray the cup-shaped skeleton of the coral polyp.

REFERENCES

Alexander, R. (2006). *Towards dialogic teaching: Rethinking classroom talk* (3rd ed.). Thirsk, UK: Dialogos.

Armbruster, B.B., & Anderson, T.H. (1988). On selecting "considerate" content area textbooks. *Remedial and Special Education, 9*(1), 47–52. doi:10.1177/074193258800900109

August, D., & Shanahan, T. (Eds.). (2006). *Developing literacy in second-language learners: Report of the National Literacy Panel on Language-Minority Children and Youth.* Mahwah, NJ: Erlbaum; Washington, DC: Center for Applied Linguistics.

Ball, D.L., Sleep, L., Boerst, T.A., & Bass, H. (2009). Combining the development of practice and the practice of development in teacher education. *The Elementary School Journal, 109*(5), 458–474. doi:10.1086/596996

Beck, I.L., & McKeown, M.G. (2006). *Improving comprehension with Questioning the Author: A fresh and expanded view of a powerful approach.* New York: Scholastic.

Beck, I.L., McKeown, M.G., Hamilton, R.L., & Kucan, L. (1997). *Questioning the Author: An approach for enhancing student engagement with text.* Newark, DE: International Reading Association.

Beck, I.L., McKeown, M.G., Sinatra, G.M., & Loxterman, J.A. (1991). Revising social studies text from a text-processing perspective: Evidence of improved comprehensibility. *Reading Research Quarterly, 26*(3), 251–276. doi:10.2307/747763

Boyd, M.P. (2012). Planning and realigning a lesson in response to student contributions. *The Elementary School Journal, 113*(1), 25–51. doi:10.1086/665817

Boyd, M.P., & Markarian, W.C. (2011). Dialogic teaching: Talk in service of a dialogic stance. *Language and Education, 25*(6), 515–534. doi:10.1080/09500782.2011.597861

Bransford, J.D., Brown, A.L., & Cocking, R.R. (Eds.). (1999). *How people learn: Brain, mind, experience, and school.* Washington, DC: National Academy Press.

Cazden, C.B. (1993). Vygotsky, Hymes, and Bakhtin: From word to utterance and voice. In E.A. Forman, N. Minick, & C.A. Stone (Eds.), *Contexts for learning: Sociocultural dynamics in children's development* (pp. 197–212). New York: Oxford University Press.

Chi, M.T.H., De Leeuw, N., Chiu, M.-H., & LaVancher, C. (1994). Eliciting self-explanations improves understanding. *Cognitive Science, 18*(3), 439–477.

Chinn, C.A., & Anderson, R.C. (1998). The structure of discussions that promote reasoning. *Teachers College Record, 100*(2), 315–368.

Clark, C.M., & Peterson, P.L. (1986). Teachers' thought processes. In M.C. Wittrock (Ed.), *Handbook of research on teaching* (3rd ed., pp. 255–296). New York: Macmillan.

Clark, H.H., & Clark, E.V. (1977). *Psychology and language: An introduction to psycholinguistics.* New York: Harcourt Brace Jovanovich.

Coleman, E.B. (1998). Using explanatory knowledge during collaborative problem solving in science. *The Journal of the Learning Sciences, 7*(3/4), 387–427.

Dewey, J. (1916). *Democracy and education: An introduction to the philosophy of education.* New York: Macmillan.

Duffy, G.G., & Hoffman, J.V. (1999). In pursuit of an illusion: The flawed search for a perfect method. *The Reading Teacher, 53*(1), 10–16.

Duke, N.K. (2000). 3.6 minutes per day: The scarcity of informational texts in first grade. *Reading Research Quarterly, 35*(2), 202–224. doi:10.1598/RRQ.35.2.1

Duke, N.K., Pearson, P.D., Strachan, S.L., & Billman, A.K. (2011). Essential elements of fostering and teaching reading comprehension. In S.J. Samuels & A.E. Farstrup (Eds.),

What research has to say about reading instruction (4th ed., pp. 51–93). Newark, DE: International Reading Association.

Fang, Z. (2006). The language demands of science reading in middle school. *International Journal of Science Education, 28*(5), 491–520. doi:10.1080/09500690500339092

Gee, J.P. (1990). *Social linguistics and literacies: Ideology in discourse.* Bristol, PA: Falmer.

Goldenberg, C. (1992). Instructional conversations: Promoting comprehension through discussion. *The Reading Teacher, 46*(4), 316–326.

Goldenberg, C., & Coleman, R. (2010). *Promoting academic achievement among English learners: A guide to the research.* Thousand Oaks, CA: Sage.

Goldenberg, C., & Patthey-Chavez, G. (1995). Discourse processes in Instructional Conversations: Interactions between teacher and transition readers. *Discourse Processes, 19*(1), 57–73. doi:10.1080/01638539109544905

Graesser, A.C., McNamara, D.S., & Kulikowich, J.M. (2011). Coh-Metrix: Providing multilevel analyses of text characteristics. *Educational Researcher, 40*(5), 223–234. doi:10.3102/0013189X11413260

Graesser, A.C., McNamara, D.S., & Louwerse, M.M. (2003). What do readers need to learn in order to process coherence relations in narrative and expository text? In A.P. Sweet & C.E. Snow (Eds.), *Rethinking reading comprehension* (pp. 82–98). New York: Guilford.

Grossman, P., Compton, C., Igra, D., Ronfeldt, M., Shahan, E., & Williamson, P. (2009). Teaching practice: A cross-professional perspective. *Teachers College Record, 111*(9), 2055–2100.

Guthrie, J.T. (2004). Teaching for literacy engagement. *Journal of Literacy Research, 36*(1), 1–29.

Heath, S.B. (1983). *Ways with words: Language, life, and work in communities and classrooms.* New York: Cambridge University Press.

Hirsch, E.D., Jr. (2006). The case for bringing content into the language arts block and for a knowledge-rich curriculum core for all children. *American Educator,* Spring. Retrieved December 13, 2012, from www.aft.org/newspubs/periodicals/ae/spring2006/hirsch.cfm

John, P.D. (2006). Lesson planning and the student teacher: Re-thinking the dominant model. *Journal of Curriculum Studies, 38*(4), 483–498. doi:10.1080/00220270500363620

King, A. (1990). Enhancing peer interaction and learning in the classroom through reciprocal questioning. *American Educational Research Journal, 27*(4), 664–687.

Kintsch, W. (1998). *Comprehension: A paradigm for cognition.* New York: Cambridge University Press.

Kintsch, W., & Rawson, K.A. (2005). Comprehension. In M.J. Snowling & C. Hulme (Eds.), *The science of reading: A handbook* (pp. 209–226). Hoboken, NJ: Wiley-Blackwell. doi:10.1002/9780470757642.ch12

Kucan, L. (2007). Insights from teachers who analyzed transcripts of their own classroom discussions. *The Reading Teacher, 61*(3), 228–236. doi:10.1598/RT.61.3.3

Kucan, L. (2009). Engaging teachers in investigating their teaching as a linguistic enterprise: The case of comprehension instruction in the context of discussion. *Reading Psychology, 30*(1), 51–87. doi:10.1080/02702710802274770

Kucan, L., & Beck, I.L. (1997). Thinking aloud and reading comprehension research: Inquiry, instruction, and social interaction. *Review of Educational Research, 67*(3), 271–299.

Kucan, L., Hapgood, S., & Palincsar, A.S. (2011). Teachers' specialized knowledge for supporting student comprehension in text-based discussions. *The Elementary School Journal, 112*(1), 61–82. doi:10.1086/660689

Kucan, L., & Palincsar, A.S. (2008–2011). *The iterative design of modules to support reading comprehension instruction* (Award No. R305A080005). Grant awarded by the Institute of Education Sciences, U.S. Department of Education.

Kucan, L., Palincsar, A.S., Busse, T., Heisey, N., Klingelhofer, R., Rimbey, M., et al. (2011). Applying the Grossman et al. theoretical framework: The case of reading. *Teachers College Record, 113*(12), 2897–2921.

Kucan, L., Palincsar, A.S., Khasnabis, D., & Chang, C.I. (2009). The video viewing task: A source of information for assessing and addressing teacher understanding of text-based discussion. *Teaching and Teacher Education, 25*(3), 415–423. doi:10.1016/j.tate.2008.09.003

Lesaux, N.K., Rupp, A.A., & Siegel, L.S. (2007). Growth in reading skills of children from diverse linguistic backgrounds: Findings from a 5-year longitudinal study. *Journal of Educational Psychology, 99*(4), 821–834. doi:10.1037/0022-0663.99.4.821

Lewis, C., Perry, R., & Murata, A. (2006). How should research contribute to instructional improvement? The case of lesson study. *Educational Researcher, 35*(3), 3–14. doi:10.3102/0013189X035003003

Litowitz, B.E. (1993). Deconstruction in the zone of proximal development. In E.A. Forman, N. Minick, & C.A. Stone (Eds.), *Contexts for learning: Sociocultural dynamics in children's development* (pp. 184–196). New York: Oxford University Press.

Manguel, A. (1996). *A history of reading.* Toronto, ON, Canada: Alfred A. Knopf.

McKeown, M.G., Beck, I.L., & Blake, R.G.K. (2009). Rethinking reading comprehension instruction: A comparison of instruction for strategies and content approaches. *Reading Research Quarterly, 44*(3), 218–253. doi:10.1598/RRQ.44.3.1

Mesmer, H.A., Cunningham, J.W., & Hiebert, E.H. (2012). Toward a theoretical model of text complexity for the early grades: Learning from the past, anticipating the future. *Reading Research Quarterly, 47*(3), 235–258.

Meyer, B.J.F., Wijekumar, K.K., & Lin, Y.-C. (2011). Individualizing a Web-based structure strategy intervention for fifth graders' comprehension of nonfiction. *Journal of Educational Psychology, 103*(1), 140–168. doi:10.1037/a0021606

Moll, L.C. (1992). Literacy research in community and classrooms: A sociocultural approach. In R. Beach, J.L. Green, M.L. Kamil, & T. Shanahan (Eds.), *Multidisciplinary perspectives on literacy research* (pp. 211–244). Urbana, IL: National Council of Teachers of English.

National Governors Association Center for Best Practices & Council of Chief State School Officers. (2010). *Common Core State Standards for English language arts and literacy in history/social studies, science, and technical subjects.* Washington, DC: Authors.

Neuman, S.B., & Celano, D. (2001). Access to print in low-income and middle-income communities: An ecological study of four neighborhoods. *Reading Research Quarterly, 36*(1), 8–26. doi:10.1598/RRQ.36.1.1

Nystrand, M. (with Gamoran, A., Kachur, R., & Prendergast, C.). (1997). *Opening dialogue: Understanding the dynamics of language and learning in the English classroom.* New York: Teachers College Press.

Palincsar, A.S. (2003). Collaborative approaches to comprehension instruction. In A.P. Sweet & C.E. Snow (Eds.), *Rethinking reading comprehension* (pp. 99–114). New York: Guilford.

Palincsar, A.S., & Brown, A.L. (1984). Reciprocal teaching of comprehension-fostering and comprehension-monitoring activities. *Cognition and Instruction, 1*(2), 117–175. doi:10.1207/s1532690xci0102_1

Palincsar, A.S., & Brown, A.L. (1989). Classroom dialogues to promote self-regulated comprehension. In J. Brophy (Ed.), *Teaching for understanding and self-regulated learning* (pp. 35–71). Greenwich, CT: JAI.

Palincsar, A.S., Magnusson, S., & Spiro, R. (2003–2006). *Investigating the feasibility of scaling up effective reading comprehension instruction using innovative video-case-based hypermedia* (Award No. 00). Grant awarded by the National Science Foundation.

Palincsar, A.S., & Schutz, K.M. (2011). Reconnecting strategy instruction with its theoretical roots. *Theory Into Practice, 50*(2), 85–92. doi:10.1080/00405841.2011.558432

Palincsar, A.S., Spiro, R.J., Kucan, L., Magnusson, S.J., Collins, B., Hapgood, S., et al. (2007). Designing a hypermedia environment to support comprehension instruction. In D.S. McNamara (Ed.), *Reading comprehension strategies: Theories, interventions, and technologies* (pp. 441–462). Mahwah, NJ: Erlbaum.

Pearson, P.D., Gallagher, M.C. (1983). The instruction of reading comprehension. *Contemporary Educational Psychology, 8*(3), 317–344.

Perfetti, C. (2011). Reading processes and reading problems: Progress toward a universal reading science. In P. McCardle, B. Miller, J.R. Lee, & O.J.L. Tzeng (Eds.), *Dyslexia across languages: Orthography and the brain–gene–behavior link* (pp. 18–32). Baltimore: Paul H. Brookes.

Pica, T. (1994). Research on negotiation: What does it reveal about second-language learning conditions, processes, and outcomes? *Language Learning, 44*(3), 493–527. doi:10.1111/j.1467-1770.1994.tb01115.x

Planty, M., Hussar, W., Snyder, T., Kena, G., KewalRamani, A., Kemp, J., et al. (2009). *The condition of education 2009* (NCES 2009-081). Washington, DC: National Center for Education Statistics, Institute of Education Sciences, U.S. Department of Education. Retrieved December 13, 2012, from nces.ed.gov/pubs2009/2009081.pdf

Pontecorvo, C. (1993). Forms of discourse and shared thinking. *Cognition and Instruction, 11*(3/4), 189–196. doi:10.1080/07370008.1993.9649019

Pressley, M., Johnson, C.J., Symons, S., McGoldrick, J.A., & Kurita, J.A. (1989). Strategies that improve children's memory and comprehension of text. *The Elementary School Journal, 90*(1), 3–32. doi:10.1086/461599

RAND Reading Study Group. (2002). *Reading for understanding: Toward an R&D program in reading comprehension.* Santa Monica, CA: RAND.

Rogoff, B. (1998). Cognition as a collaborative process. In W. Damon, (Series. Ed.), D. Kuhn, & R.S. Siegler (Vol. Eds.), *Cognition, perception, and language: Vol. 2. Handbook of child psychology* (5th ed., pp. 679–744). New York: Wiley.

Rosaen, C.L., Schram, P., & Herbel-Eisenmann, B. (2002). Using hypermedia technology to explore connections among mathematics, language, and literacy in teacher education. *Contemporary Issues in Technology and Teacher Education, 2*(3), 297–326.

Roschelle, J. (1992). Learning by collaborating: Convergent conceptual change. *The Journal of the Learning Sciences, 2*(3), 235–276.

Schleppegrell, M.J. (2001). Linguistic features of the language of schooling. *Linguistics and Education, 12*(4), 431–459. doi:10.1016/S0898-5898(01)00073-0

Schleppegrell, M.J. (2004). *The language of schooling: A functional linguistics perspective.* Mahwah, NJ: Erlbaum.

Sherin, M.G. (2004). New perspectives on the role of video in teacher education. In J. Brophy (Ed.), *Using video in teacher education* (pp. 1–27). Bingley, UK: Emerald. doi:10.1016/S1479-3687(03)10001-6

Steele, C.M. (1992). Race and the schooling of black Americans. *The Atlantic, 269*(4), 68–78.

U.S. Department of Education. (2009). *The Nation's Report Card: Reading 2009* (NCES 2010-458). Washington, DC: National Center for Education Statistics, Institute of Education Sciences, U.S. Department of Education.

Van Den Branden, K. (2000). Does negotiation of meaning promote reading comprehension? A study of multilingual primary school classes. *Reading Research Quarterly, 35*(3), 426–443. doi:10.1598/RRQ.35.3.6

van den Broek, P., Rapp, D.N., & Kendeou, P. (2005). Integrating memory-based and constructionist processes in accounts of reading comprehension. *Discourse Processes, 39*(2/3), 299–316.

van den Broek, P., Risden, K., Fletcher, C.R., & Thurlow, R. (1996). A "landscape" view of reading: Fluctuating patterns of activation and the construction of a stable memory representation. In B.K. Britton & A.C. Graesser (Eds.), *Models of understanding text* (pp. 165–187). Mahwah, NJ: Erlbaum.

van den Broek, P., Young, M., Tzeng, Y., & Linderholm, T. (1999). The landscape model of reading: Inferences and the online construction of memory representation. In H. van Oostendorp & S.R. Goldman (Eds.), *The construction of mental representations during reading* (pp. 62–87). Mahwah, NJ: Erlbaum.

Vygotsky, L.S. (1978). *Mind in society: The development of higher psychological processes* (M. Cole, V. John-Steiner, S. Scribner, E. Souberman, Eds. & Trans.). Cambridge, MA: Harvard University Press.

Vygotsky, L.S. (1986). *Thought and language* (A. Kozulin, Trans.). Cambridge, MA: MIT Press. (Original work published 1934)

Wilkinson, I.A.G., & Son, E.H. (2011). A dialogic turn in research on learning and teaching to comprehend. In M.L. Kamil, P.D. Pearson, E.B. Moje, & P.P. Afflerbach (Eds.), *Handbook of reading research* (Vol. 4, pp. 359–387). New York: Routledge.

Wilkinson, I.A.G., Soter, A.O., & Murphy, P.K. (2010). Developing a model of quality talk about literary text. In M.G. McKeown & L. Kucan (Eds.), *Bringing reading research to life* (pp. 142–169). New York: Guilford.

Wittrock, M.C. (Ed.). (1986). *Handbook of research on teaching* (3rd ed.). New York: Macmillan.

Wolf, M.K., Crosson, A.C., & Resnick, L.B. (2005). Classroom talk for rigorous reading comprehension instruction. *Reading Psychology, 26*(1), 27–53. doi:10.1080/02702710490897518

Zahorik, J.A. (1970). The effect of planning on teaching. *The Elementary School Journal, 71*(3), 143–151. doi:10.1086/460625